MW00587568

DEVOTIONS
FOR DEALING
WITH ANXIETY

DEVOTIONS FOR DEALING WITH ANXIETY

100 Meditations for Men

CHARLES SPURGEON

BARBOUR
PUBLISHING

© 2024 by Barbour Publishing, Inc.

Editorial assistance by Elijah Adkins.

ISBN 978-1-63609-978-1

All rights reserved. No part of this publication may be reproduced or transmitted for commercial purposes, except for brief quotations in printed reviews, without written permission of the publisher. Reproduced text may not be used on the World Wide Web. No Barbour Publishing content may be used as artificial intelligence training data for machine learning, or in any similar software development.

Churches and other noncommercial interests may reproduce portions of this book without the express written permission of Barbour Publishing, provided that the text does not exceed 500 words and that the text is not material quoted from another publisher. When reproducing text from this book, include the following credit line: "From *Devotions for Dealing with Anxiety*, published by Barbour Publishing, Inc. Used by permission."

All scripture quotations are taken from the King James Version of the Bible.

Cover Design: Greg Jackson, Thinkpen Design

Published by Barbour Publishing, Inc., 1810 Barbour Drive, Uhrichsville, Ohio 44683, www.barbourbooks.com

Our mission is to inspire the world with the life-changing message of the Bible.

Printed in China.

INTRODUCTION

Even in anxiety, there is hope.

Charles Spurgeon, "the Prince of Preachers," is well remembered and remarkably readable some 130 years after his death. Though he was a beloved and highly successful minister of the gospel—he pastored a "megachurch" in London a century before the term came into use—Spurgeon himself often struggled with dark thoughts. Like Jesus, whom he served so faithfully, Charles Spurgeon could be "touched with the feeling of our infirmities" (Hebrews 4:15).

At the Mildmay Park Conference in 1890, Spurgeon said, "Darkness—can it fall upon a child of God? He is a child of light—shall he walk in darkness? Not darkness in the sense of ignorance and sin and death, but in the sense of gloom and sorrow. Saints may have much of it. The heir of heaven sometimes knows a midnight. But if he is with Jesus, following Him as his leader, then he is in a safe condition."

This new devotional is compiled from Spurgeon's decades of weekly sermons and other teachings. On the following pages, you'll find spiritually deep but personally accessible teaching on anxiety and its related challenges, including fear and depression. Spurgeon had an unparalleled way of distilling godly principles for living, and here he deals with the voices that nag at our minds and hold us back from the life God would have us live.

Covering the sources, impact, and management of anxiety,

these one hundred entries will bring powerful scriptural truths to bear on the topic. Spurgeon's text has been only lightly updated for spelling and punctuation, and each reading is accompanied by a brief description of its origin.

Devotions for Dealing with Anxiety is a powerful, needful book for our times.

FEARING FOR THE FUTURE

Casting all your care upon him; for he careth for you.
1 Peter 5:7

One of the first and most natural cares with which we are vexed is the care for daily bread. "I should be content," says one, "with food and raiment. If I can but provide things honest in the sight of all men, and see my family cared for, I shall then be happy." "But," saith one, "what shall I eat, what shall I drink, wherewithal shall I be clothed? Without a situation, having therefore no opportunity to earn my livelihood; without substance, having therefore nothing to look upon by which I may be supported without labor; without friend or patron who might give me his generous assistance, what shall I do?"

You are a Christian, are you? You must use all diligence, that is your duty. But oh, if God shall help you, mingle no fretfulness with the diligence, no impatience with your suffering, and no distrust with your trials.

No, remember what Jesus has said so sweetly to the point: "Behold the fowls of the air: for they sow not, neither do they reap, nor gather into barns; yet your heavenly Father feedeth them. Are ye not much better than they? Which of you by taking thought can add one cubit unto his stature? And why take ye thought for raiment? Consider the lilies of the field, how they grow; they toil not, neither do they spin: and yet I say unto you, That even Solomon in his glory was not arrayed like one of these. . . . Therefore take no thought, saying, What shall we eat? or, What shall we drink? or, Wherewithal shall we be clothed? (for after all these things do the Gentiles seek:) for your heavenly Father knoweth that ye have need of all these things. But seek ye first the kingdom of God, and his righteousness; and all these things shall be added unto you."

Such a care as that I say is natural enough, and to bid a man shake it off when he is in actual need is cruelly absurd, unless you have a sure consolation to offer him. But you can say, "Cast your trial upon God." Use your most earnest endeavors; humble yourself under the mighty hand of God.

"A Cure for Care," Metropolitan Tabernacle Pulpit, No. 428 (1862)

THE WORST TYPE OF WORRY

*Blessed is the man that trusteth in the
LORD, and whose hope the LORD is.*
JEREMIAH 17:7

But each Christian will in his time have personal troubles of a higher order, namely, spiritual cares. He is begotten again unto a lively hope, but he fears that his faith will yet die. He hopes he has some spark of spiritual joy, but there are dark and dreary nights which lower over him, and he fears that his lamp will die out in darkness.

Beloved, I beseech you, cast this care upon God, for He careth for you. "I am persuaded that he that hath begun a good work in you will carry it on and perfect it unto the day of Christ." He has said, "I will never leave thee, nor forsake thee." "The mountains shall depart, and the hills be removed; but my kindness shall not depart from thee, neither shall the covenant of my peace be removed, saith the LORD that hath mercy on thee."

Away then with dark suspicions and anxieties! Is it care about past sin? "The blood of Jesus Christ, God's dear Son, cleanseth us from all sin." Is it present temptation? "There hath no temptation happened to you but such as is common to men: but God who is faithful, who will not suffer you to be tempted above that ye are able; but will with the temptation also make a way to escape, that ye may be able to bear it." Is it future peril? O leave you that with Him, for neither "things present, nor things to come, nor height, nor depth, nor any other creature, shall be able to separate us from the love of God, which is in Christ Jesus our Lord."

If you begin to think always of yourself, you must be miserable. Why, it is Christ that makes you what you are before the eyes of God. Look then to Jesus in order to find out what you are in God's esteem. Soul, I say again, look at Christ, and not at yourself. Never let anxieties about sanctification destroy your confidence of justification. What if you be a sinner! Christ died to save sinners. What if you be undeserving! "In due time Christ died for the ungodly." Grace is free. The invitation is still open to you. Rest the whole burden of your soul's salvation where it must rest.

"A CURE FOR CARE," METROPOLITAN
TABERNACLE PULPIT, No. 428 (1862)

HOPEFUL PROMISES

*Thou wilt keep him in perfect peace, whose mind
is stayed on thee: because he trusteth in thee.*
ISAIAH 26:3

Believe in a universal providence: the Lord cares for ants and angels, for worms and for worlds. He cares for cherubim and for sparrows, for seraphim and for insects. Cast your care on Him, He that calleth the stars by their names and leadeth them out by numbers, by their hosts.

"Why sayest thou, O Jacob, and thinkest, O Israel, my way is passed over from God and He has utterly forgotten me?" Let His universal providence cheer you. Think next of His particular providence over all the saints. "Precious shall their blood be in his sight." "Precious in the sight of the LORD is the death of his saints." "We know that all things work together for good to them that love God, to them that are the called according to his purpose." Let the fact that while He is the Savior of all men, He is specially the Savior of them that believe. Let that cheer and comfort you, that special providence which watches over the chosen: "The angel of the LORD encampeth round about them that fear him." And then thirdly, let the thought of His special love to you be the very essence of your comfort. "I will never leave thee, nor forsake thee." God says that as much to you as He said it to any saint of old. "Fear not, I am thy shield, and thy exceeding great reward."

Oh! I would, beloved, that the Holy Ghost would make you feel the promise as being spoken to you. Out of this vast assembly forget the rest and only think of yourself, for the promises are unto you, meant for you. Oh! Grasp them. It is ill to get into a way of reading scripture for the whole church—read it for yourselves and specially hear the Master say to you this morning, "Let not your heart be troubled: ye believe in God, believe also in me." Think that you hear Him say, "I have prayed for thee that thy faith fail not." Think you see Him walking on the waters of your trouble, for He is there and He is saying, "Fear not, it is I; be not afraid."

"A Cure for Care," Metropolitan Tabernacle Pulpit, No. 428 (1862)

ABOUNDING IN JOY

But let all those that put their trust in thee rejoice:
let them ever shout for joy, because thou defendest them:
let them also that love thy name be joyful in thee.
PSALM 5:11

Listen to the following line of argument, which shall be very brief. You only act reasonably when you rejoice. If you are chosen of God and redeemed by blood and have been made an heir of heaven, you ought to rejoice. We pray you, act not contrary to nature and reason. Do not fly in the face of great and precious truths. From what you profess, you are bound to be joyful. You will best baffle your adversaries by being happy.

"They say, they say"—let them say! "Rest in the LORD, and wait patiently for him." But the attack is cruel. No doubt it is, but the Lord knows all about it. Do not cease to rest in Him. If your heart is full of God's love, you can easily bear all that the enemy may cast upon you. Abound in joy, for then you will behave best to those who are round about you.

One of the best specifics for good temper is communion with God and consequent joy of heart. You yourself also, if you are happy, will be strong: "The joy of the LORD is your strength." If you lose your joy in your religion, you will be a poor worker, you cannot bear strong testimony, you cannot bear stern trial, you cannot lead a powerful life. In proportion as you maintain your joy, you will be strong *in* the Lord, and *for* the Lord.

With joy we rehearse the song of songs. We pay glad homage now before Jehovah's throne. We sing unto the Lord our gladsome harmonies, and we will do so as long as we have any being. Pass me that score, O chief musician of the skies, for I can take it up and sing my part in bass, or tenor, or treble, or alto, or soprano, as my voice may be. The key is joy in God. Whatever the part assigned us, the music is all for Jesus.

"JOY, JOY FOR EVER," METROPOLITAN TABERNACLE PULPIT, NO. 2146 (1890)

GRIEVOUS
SELF-REFLECTION

Peter was grieved because he said unto
him the third time, Lovest thou me?
JOHN 21:17

Peter may have thought to himself, *Why does my Lord ask me*
three times? It may be I am deluded, and that I do not love Him.
Before his fall he would have said, "Lord, Thou knowest that
I love Thee, how canst Thou ask me? Have I not proved it?
Did I not step down into the sea at Thy beck and call? I will
go through fire and water for Thee." But Simon, son of Jonas,
had learned to be more sober and less loud in his protests.
He had been tried, he had attempted to stand alone—and
he had proved his palpable weakness.

A burned child is afraid of fire, and a scalded child
shudders at hot water. So a precocious Peter feels the peril
of presumption. His timidity troubles him. He hesitates to
give his word of honor. Distrust of self distresses him. He
dreams his former downfall o'er and o'er again. The hypoc-
risy of his own heart horrifies him. What can he say? He
answers the accuser, or rather he appeals to the appellant:
"Thou knowest all things; Thou knowest that I love Thee."
His previous guilt causes his present grief.

Should like horrors haunt you, friends, give no place to
grievous misgivings. Do not encourage them. Hie away to

the cross; behold the thorny crown. Fly at once, poor guilty sinner, to the great atonement which was made by the Lord upon the tree, and let that fear be ended once for all. Because of the tenacity of his love, Peter was grieved. Had he not loved Christ so ardently, he would not have felt the grief so acutely.

I tell some of our dear young people who get into trouble and say they are afraid that they are hypocrites that I never yet knew a hypocrite who said he was afraid he was one—and those who say that they are afraid they do not love Jesus and are timid and trembling (though I do not commend them for their trembling) yet I have a much better hope of some of them than I have of others who are loud in their protests and vehement in asserting, "Though all men forsake Thee, yet will not I."

"Do I Love the Lord or No?" Metropolitan Tabernacle Pulpit, No. 3524 (Undated)

WHEN NIGHT FALLS

Now from the sixth hour there was darkness
over all the land unto the ninth hour.
MATTHEW 27:45

Another practical lesson is this: if we are in the dark at this time, if our spirits are sunk in gloom, let us not despair, for the Lord Christ Himself was there. If I have fallen into misery on account of sin, let me not give up all hope, for the Father's Well-beloved passed through denser darkness than mine.

O believing soul, if you are in the dark you are near the King's cellars, and there are wines on the lees well refined lying there. You have gotten into the pavilion of the Lord, and now may you speak with Him. You will not find Christ in the gaudy tents of pride, nor in the foul haunts of wickedness; you will not find Him where the viol and the dance and the flowing bowl inflame the lusts of men—but in the house of mourning you will meet the Man of Sorrows. He is not where Herodias dances, nor where Bernice displays her charms, but He is where the woman of a sorrowful spirit moves her lips in prayer. He is never absent where penitence sits in darkness and bewails her faults:

> *Yes, Lord, in hours of gloom,*
> *When shadows fill my room,*
> *When pain breathes forth its groans,*

And grief its sighs and moans,
Then You are near.

If you are under a cloud, feel after your Lord, if perhaps you may find Him. Stand still in your black sorrow, and say, "O Lord, the preacher tells me that Your cross once stood in such darkness as this—O Jesus, hear me!" He will respond to you; the Lord will look out of the pillar of cloud, and shed a light upon you. "I know their sorrows," He says. He is no stranger to heartbreak. Christ also once suffered for sin. Trust Him, and He will cause His light to shine upon you. Lean upon Him, and He will bring you up out of the gloomy wilderness into the land of rest.

If you have found my Lord, I charge you never let Him go, but cleave to Him till the day break and the shadows flee away. God help you so to do for Jesus' sake!

"The Three Hours of Darkness," Metropolitan
Tabernacle Pulpit, No. 1896 (1886)

UPS AND DOWNS

And Manoah said unto his wife, We shall
surely die, because we have seen God.
JUDGES 13:22

Some of us have learned to be afraid of joy. Sadness is often the herald of satisfaction, but bliss is oftentimes the harbinger of pain. How strangely is it related of our Lord! He went into the Jordan of His baptism, the Spirit descended upon Him like a dove, the Father's voice saluted Him: "Thou art my beloved Son in whom I am well pleased." What next? "And immediately the Spirit driveth him into the wilderness: and he was there in the wilderness forty days tempted of Satan, and was with the wild beasts."

God does not give His people weapons to play with. He does not give them strength to spend on their lusts. Lord, if You have given me these goodly weapons, it is sure I shall need them in hard fighting. If I have had a feast at Your table, I will remember that it is but a short walk from the upper chamber to the garden of Gethsemane.

Daniel, the man greatly beloved, was reduced very low. "All his comeliness was turned into corruption and he retained no strength," when God showed him "the great vision." Thus too, with favored John, he must be banished to Patmos; in the deep solitude of that Aegean sea–girt island he must receive "the Revelation of Jesus Christ which God gave unto him." I have noticed, in the ordinary scenes of Christian experience, that our greatest joys come just after some of our sorest trials. When the howling tempest has played out its strength, it soothes itself to sleep. Then comes a season of calm and quiet, so profound in its stillness that only the monstrous tempest could have been the mother of so mighty a calm.

So seems it with us. Deep waves of trial, high mountains of joy—but the reverse is almost as often true: from Pisgah's top we go to our graves; from the top of Carmel we have to go down to the dens of lion and fight with the leopards. Let us be on our watchtower, lest like Manoah, having seen the angel of God, the next thing should be that we say we shall surely die, for we have seen the Lord.

"Cheer for the Faint-Hearted," Metropolitan Tabernacle Pulpit, No. 440 (1862)

IT HELPS TO REMEMBER

But his wife said unto him, If the LORD were pleased
to kill us, he would not have received a burnt offering
and a meat offering at our hands, neither would
he have shewed us all these things, nor would as
at this time have told us such things as these.
JUDGES 13:23

"These are hard times!" Times have always been hard ever since I recollect them, and I suppose they ever will be, for they used to be hard in our grandfathers' days, and there seems to be no likelihood but what they will continue to be so. The present is what we have got in hand; let us make the right use of it.

But you have had losses and crosses and disappointments. You are chastened every morning and you are troubled all day long, and Satan whispered to you last Saturday night, when you were putting up the shutters as tired as you could be, "It is no use going to the house of God tomorrow. There is nothing there for you. God has been troubling you all week. He means to destroy you. He is going to give you up. You may do what you will, but the current is too strong. You may tug and pull, but you will starve for all that. God has forsaken you, and your enemies are persecuting you on every side."

Well, now, it would be a very curious thing if it were true.

But it is not true, for the reasons which Manoah's wife gave. You know that when your faith laid hold of Christ, God did not spurn the sacrifice you brought. When you said, for the first time in your life,

> *My faith doth lay her hand*
> *On that dear head of Thine,*
> *While like a penitent I stand,*
> *And here confess my sin,*

He did not reject the offering which you then presented to Him, but He spoke with loving voice and said, "Go and sin no more. Thy sins, which are many, are all forgiven thee."

In looking back upon the past, you can remember many times and seasons when God has especially answered you as though He would rend the heavens and put out His right hand full of the mercies which you needed.

"**Cheer for the Faint-Hearted**," **Metropolitan Tabernacle Pulpit**, No. 440 (1862)

HOPE IN DESPERATION

For I know the thoughts that I think toward
you, saith the LORD, thoughts of peace,
and not of evil, to give you an expected end.
JEREMIAH 29:11

Nay, soul, thus says the Lord to you: "Was there not a time when Christ was precious to you?" O backslider, was there not a season when you could put your finger into the prints of the nails, and your hand into His side? Poor fallen soul, was there not a period when that precious hymn of Toplady's was sweet to your ears?—

Nothing in my hands I bring,
Simply to Thy cross I cling;
Naked, look to Thee for dress,
Helpless, come to Thee for grace;
Black I to the fountain fly,
Wash me, Savior, or I die.

Then I tell you, soul, if the Lord had ever meant to destroy you, He would never have permitted you to know a precious Christ or to put your trust in Him. Besides, fallen though you now are, through sore travail, yet was there not a time when you saw the beauty of God in His temple? I went to the house of God with the company that kept holy day; His name to me was as ointment poured forth. My soul delighted herself in her God, and my spirit made her boast in her King. O Jesus, once You were very sweet to me. I knew the plague of my own heart even then, but I knew Your power to save. I knew the fellowship of the Father and of His Son, Jesus Christ:

> *What peaceful hours I then enjoyed,*
> *How sweet their memory still!*
> *But they have left an aching void,*
> *The world can never fill.*

Our soul! What a mercy it is that the world cannot fill it, and what a greater mercy still that God will fill it—for He never emptied a soul He did not mean to fill. He never stripped a man He did not mean to clothe; He never made one a spiritual beggar without intending to make him spiritually rich. And if you tonight are brought to the first stage of desperation, you are brought to the first stage of hope. Now that man comes to his wit's end, God shall begin to magnify His mercy and His truth.

"Cheer for the Faint-Hearted," Metropolitan Tabernacle Pulpit, No. 440 (1862)

PRAYERS IN A CAVE

Maschil of David: A prayer when he was in the cave.
<small>TITLE OF PSALM 142</small>

David did pray when he was in the cave. If he had prayed half as much when he was in the palace as he did when he was in the cave, it would have been better for him. But alas! When he was king, we find him rising from his bed in the evening and looking from the roof of the house and falling into temptation. If he had been looking up to heaven, if his heart had been in communion with God, he might never have committed that great crime which has so deeply stained his whole character.

"A prayer when he was in the cave." God will hear prayer on land and on the sea and even under the sea. Our God is not the God of the hills only but of the valleys also; He is God of both sea and land. He heard Jonah when the disobedient prophet was at the bottom of the mountains, and the earth with her bars seemed to be about him forever. Wherever you work, you can pray. Wherever you lie sick, you can pray. There is no place to which you can be banished where God is not near, and there is no time of day or night when His throne is inaccessible.

"A prayer when he was in the cave." The caves have heard the best prayers. Some birds sing best in cages. I have heard that some of God's people shine brightest in the dark.

There is many an heir of heaven who never prays so well as when he is driven by necessity to pray. Some shall sing aloud upon their beds of sickness, whose voices were hardly heard when they were well, and some shall sing God's high praises in the fire who did not praise Him as they should before the trial came. In the furnace of affliction the saints are often seen at their best.

If any of you tonight are in dark and gloomy positions, if your souls are bowed down within you, may this become a special time for peculiarly prevalent communion and intercession—and may the prayer of the cave be the very best of your prayers!

"DAVID'S PRAYER IN THE CAVE," METROPOLITAN
TABERNACLE PULPIT, NO. 2282 (1890)

HE DOESN'T FORGET

How long wilt thou forget me, O Lord? for
ever? how long wilt thou hide thy face from me?
How long shall I take counsel in my soul, having
sorrow in my heart daily? how long shall mine
enemy be exalted over me? . . . I will sing unto the
Lord, because he hath dealt bountifully with me.
Psalm 13:1–2, 6

"How long wilt thou forget me, O Lord? for ever?" Think for
a minute. Can God forget? Can omnipotence forget? Can
unchanging love forget? Can infinite faithfulness forget? Yet
so it seems to David. So it has often seemed to men in the
deepest of trouble. "How long wilt thou forget me?"

You have been praying for mercy and you cannot find
it—and you think that God forgets. You have been, perhaps,
a seeker after peace for years, and yet you have not found it,
and you think that God forgets. Or, perhaps, years ago you
were one of the happiest of the happy and you bathed in the
light of God's countenance. And now you are the unhappi-
est of the unhappy—you are at a distance from your God,
you have been trying to get back and cannot get back, and
you think that God forgets you. Or else wave upon wave of
trouble has rolled over you—you have hardly had time to
breathe between the surges of your grief. You are ready to
perish with despondency, and you think that God forgets you.

That is how it looks to you, but it is not so and cannot be so. God cannot forget anything—it is impossible. "Can a woman forget her sucking child?" Mark that expression, the child that still draws its nourishment from her bosom. That is just what you are doing still, for albeit you think that God forgets you, you are still living on what He daily gives you and you would die if He did not give you of His grace and strength. "Can a woman forget her sucking child, that she should not have compassion on the son of her womb? yea, they may forget, yet will I not forget thee." Lay hold of that great truth and dismiss that which can be only an appearance and an error. God has not forgotten to be gracious, nor has He even forgotten you.

"Howling Changed to Singing," Metropolitan Tabernacle Pulpit, No. 2310 (1889)

KEEP SEEKING GOD

But if from thence thou shalt seek the LORD
thy God, thou shalt find him, if thou seek him
with all thy heart and with all thy soul.
DEUTERONOMY 4:29

Are you crying tonight, "Lord, how long wilt Thou hide Thy face from me?" I am glad you cry about it. The ungodly do not cry for God's face to be revealed to them—they wish that God would always hide His face from them. They do not want either His face or His favor. But if you are longing to see His face, it is because that face is full of love to you.

Oh, dear child of God, if you have lost the light of your Father's countenance and you sigh after it, you shall have it again—you shall have it very soon! By the degree of your longing, you may measure the length of His absence. If you long but little, He will be absent long. But if you long much, He will soon come to you. You will soon find that the hidings of His face are over and the light of His countenance is again your joy.

This is what the trouble really is, and a great trouble it is while it lasts, though it works for your good. What plants would grow if it were always day? Does not night make them grow as well as day? Brethren, if we always had fine weather, should we ever have a harvest at all? The Arabs have a proverb: "All sun makes the desert." If there is no rain, how can there be verdure?

There is a ripeness given to the fruits by the moon as well as by the sun. Grieve when God hides His face from you, but do not despair as well as grieve but believe that even in this, He loves you still. It is a face of love that you do not see. You believe that, yourself, or else you would not wish to see it. If it were a face of wrath, you would not be longing to see it again. It is a face of love that is hidden from you. Wherefore, be of good courage—you shall see it by and by.

"HOWLING CHANGED TO SINGING," METROPOLITAN
TABERNACLE PULPIT, NO. 2310 (1889)

GUILT-FREE GRACE

Yet surely I know that it shall be well with them
that fear God, which fear before him.
ECCLESIASTES 8:12

There are some of God's best children who always grow in the shade of fear and can scarcely attain to so much as to say, "I know whom I have believed." Darkness suits them best. Their eyes are weak and much sunlight seems to blind them. They love the shadows. And though they thought they could sing, "I know my Savior, I love Him, and He loves me," they go back again, and begin to groan in themselves: "Do I love the Lord? Indeed, if it be so, why am I thus?"

Now, I am now about to utter a great paradox—I believe that some of these poor fearing people have got the greatest faith of anybody in the world. I have sometimes thought that great fear, great anxiety, must have great faith with it to keep the soul alive at all.

We sometimes think ourselves proud and we are never more humble than when we feel that we are proud. At other times, we think ourselves to be wonderfully humble and we are never more proud than then. We sometimes say within ourselves, "Now I think I am overcoming my corruptions." That is just the time when they are about to attack us most severely. At another time we are crying, "Surely I shall be cut off." That is just the period when sin is being routed, because we are hating it the most and crying out the most against it.

We are not qualified to judge ourselves—our poor scales are so out of order that they will never tell the truth. Now, then, just give up your own judgment, except thus far: Can you say that you "are a poor sinner and nothing at all and that Jesus Christ is your all in all"? Then be comforted. You have no right to be anxious. You have no reason to be so. You could not say that if you had not been converted.

You must have been quickened by grace or else you would not be anxious at all. And you must have faith or else you would not be able even to lay hold of Christ so much as to know your own nothingness and His all-sufficiency. Poor soul! Be comforted.

"FIVE FEARS," THE NEW PARK STREET
PULPIT, NO. 148 (1857)

YOU'RE NOT ALONE

Now when John had heard in the prison the works of
Christ, he sent two of his disciples, and said unto him,
Art thou he that should come, or do we look for another?
MATTHEW 11:2–3

But shall I tell you one thing? Do you know the greatest
of God's people are often in the same condition as you are
now? "No, no," says the fearful soul, "I do not believe that.
I believe that when persons are converted they never have
any fear." And they look at the minister and they say, "Oh,
but if I could be but like that minister. I know he never
has doubts and fears. Oh, if I could be like old Deacon So
and So—such a holy man, how he prays! Oh, if I could feel
like Mr. So and So, who calls to visit me and talks to me so
sweetly. They never doubt."

Ah, that is because you do not know. Those whom you
think to be the strongest (and are so in public) have their times
of the greatest weakness when they can scarcely know their
own names in spiritual things. If one may speak for the rest,
those of us who enjoy the greatest portions of assurance have
times when we would give all the world to know ourselves to
be possessors of grace. When we would be ready to sacrifice
our lives if we might but have the shadow of a hope that we
were in the love of Jesus Christ our Lord.

Now, little one, if the giants go there, what wonder if

the dwarfs must? What if God's favorite and chosen ones, what if His valiant men, the bodyguard of Christ, those men whose swords are on their thighs and who stand up for the truth and are its champions—if they sometimes are weak, what wonder if you should be weak?

What if the heirs of salvation and the soldiers of the cross sometimes feel their knees feeble and their hands hang down and their hearts faint—what wonder if you, who are less than the least of all saints, should sometimes be in trouble too?

"Doubts and fears," said an old preacher once, "are like the toothache—nothing more painful, but never fatal." They may distress us much, but they will never burn the soul.

<hr>

"FIVE FEARS," THE NEW PARK STREET
PULPIT, NO. 148 (1857)

34

BEYOND OUR ABILITY

Fear not, thou worm Jacob, and ye men of
Israel; I will help thee, saith the LORD,
and thy redeemer, the Holy One of Israel.
ISAIAH 41:14

Now the Christian may remember that, little though he be, God is with him. God will help him and that right early. Brethren, I like a man who, when he begins to do anything, is afraid of himself and says, "It is of no use. I cannot do it." Let him alone—he will do it. He is all right.

The man who says, "Oh there is nothing in it—I can do it," will break down to a dead certainty. But let him begin by saying, "I know what I am at, and I feel confident I cannot do it unless I have something more given to me than I feel today"—that man will come back with flying banners, the trumpets proclaiming that he has been victorious.

But it must be because he puts reliance upon help promised. Now, Christian, I see you this morning ready to run away from the battle. You have been so dispirited this last week, through many divers adverse circumstances, that you are ready to give up your religion. Now, man, here is a brother comrade who is passing through the same.

He comes here this morning, half inclined to run off to Tarshish like Jonah did of old, only he could not find a boat or else he might have sailed away. And he has come here to pat you on the shoulder and say, "Brother, do not let you and I play deserters, after all. Let us up to arms and still fight for our Master, for the promise says, 'I will help thee.'"

Brother, what an all-sufficient promise that is—"I will help thee." Why, it matters not what God has given us to do—if He helps us we can do it. Give me God to help me and I will split the world in halves and shiver it till it shall be smaller than the dust of the threshing floor. Ay, and if God be with me, this breath could blow whole worlds about as the child blows a bubble.

There is no saying what man can do when God is with him. Give God to a man and he can do all things.

"Fear Not," The New Park
Street Pulpit, No. 156 (1857)

36

FEAR IS UNNECESSARY

There is no fear in love; but perfect love casteth out fear: because fear hath torment. He that feareth is not made perfect in love.

1 JOHN 4:18

Brethren, you and I can do nothing of ourselves—we are poor puny things. But let us attempt great things—for God is with us. Let us dare great things, for God will not leave us.

Remember what He has done aforetime—and remember what He has done of old He will do again. Remember David the shepherd boy. Think you well of Shamgar, with his oxgoad. Forget you not the jawbone of the ass and the stone from the sling. If these worked wonders, why should not we? If little things have done great things, let us try to do great things also.

You know not, you atoms, but that your destiny is sublime. Try and make it so by faith. And the least of you may be mighty through the strength of God. Oh, for grace to trust God—and there is no telling what you can do.

Worms, you are nothing but you have eaten princes. Worms, you are nothing but you have devoured the roots of cedars and laid them level with the earth. Worms, you are nothing but you have piled rocks in the deep, deep sea and wrecked mighty navies. Worms, you have eaten through the keel of the proudest ship that ever sailed the ocean. If you have done this, yourselves, what cannot we do?

Your strength lies in your mouths—our strength lies in ours too. We will use our mouths in prayer and in constant adoration, and we shall yet conquer—for God is with us and victory is sure.

Ye trembling souls! dismiss your fears;
Be mercy all your theme:
Mercy, which, like a river, flows
In one continued stream.

Fear not that He will e'er forsake,
Or leave His work undone;
He's faithful to His promises—
And faithful to His Son.

"FEAR NOT," THE NEW PARK
STREET PULPIT, No. 156 (1857)

ESCAPING DOUBTS

Shake thyself from the dust; arise, and sit down,
O Jerusalem: loose thyself from the bands of
thy neck, O captive daughter of Zion.
ISAIAH 52:2

Let me also remind any Christian here, full of doubt and with the bands of his neck tight upon him, that the blood has not changed its power to cleanse. If it cleansed you twenty years ago, it can cleanse you still. Remember, Jesus has not lost His power to save, nor has He changed His character for willingness to save to the uttermost.

> *Jesus sits on Zion's hill,*
> *He receives poor sinners still.*

Do I hear thee say, "But I am not fit to come back to Christ, and have joy in Him at once"? Oh! Sir, wert thou fit at first? No, and thou art not fit now—but come and welcome. Christ wants naught from thee. Come and trust Him and perfect salvation is thine. "Oh! But I cannot bear to look Him in the face, for I have lived so long without walking in His counsel." So much the more reason that thou shouldest not live another hour without Him.

I charge thee, my poor distressed brother—I charge thee, my troubled sister—by the love that Christ hath to thee, come to Him now. Behold He stands at the door and knocks. If thou wilt open to Him, though the house be not furnished nor the table covered with a festival for Him as it should be, yet will He come in and sup with thee—even with thee—and thou shalt sup with Him tonight.

I see no reason why the most desponding Christian here should not rejoice before he comes to the table of the Lord. I do not know why the most barren among us should not be made fruitful. This I do know, that we are not straitened in Him; we are not straitened in His willingness to bless nor in His ability to comfort. Oh! Believe in Him, Christian, believe Him. If thou be not a Christian, cast thyself at His feet. He will not let thee perish. Lay hold, if it be but of the skirts of His garment, and do not let Him go. Do thou even now shake thyself from the dust and put on thy beautiful garments.

"A Call to the Depressed," Metropolitan Tabernacle Pulpit, No. 3422 (Undated)

DELIVERANCE IS COMING

O thou afflicted, tossed with tempest, and not comforted, behold, I will lay thy stones with fair colours, and lay thy foundations with sapphires. And I will make thy windows of agates, and thy gates of carbuncles, and all thy borders of pleasant stones.
Isaiah 54:11–12

Perhaps you feel you cannot be comforted on earth—then you are in a fair way to get deliverance for you shall be comforted by the God of heaven. If your sore is such that no plaster of man could ever cure it, glory be to God—for blessed be His name, He delights to find those cases which baffle all human skill. There shall be seen the power of His grace, and then will He send His Word and heal you.

Every Christian will, I think, join with me in confessing that the dealings of the Lord with us have always baffled our own understanding, until we have been brought to see the end of the Lord, as Job saw it, that the Lord is full of pity and of tender mercy. Our heaviest losses have thus enriched us with our choicest gains. The things which, as they happened, caused us the most terror have fallen out to the furtherance of our best interests—and in the same manner, I believe, the more you feel the burden of sin, the majesty of the law, and the inflexible claims of divine justice, the sweeter afterwards will be your apprehension of guilt removed by the blood of

Christ, of the law fulfilled by His obedience, and of justice satisfied by His suretyship.

Take heart now, O you afflicted ones, tossed with tempest and not comforted. Pour no fresh bitters into your cup by murmuring against God and repining at His dispensations. Rather cry mightily and pray earnestly, that the God who has made your experience tally with the first verse of the text may give you to realize the fullness of that recompense which is promised in the next verse. And so shall your sighs be turned into songs. So shall you sing with David, "Thou which hast showed me great and sore troubles shalt quicken me again, and bring me up again from the depths of the earth. Thou shalt increase my greatness, and comfort me on every side." Happy day, dear soul, when you are delivered from this first storm.

"SANCTIFIED SORROW," METROPOLITAN
TABERNACLE PULPIT, NO. 3435 (UNDATED)

A WORTHWHILE REWARD

*But as it is written, Eye hath not seen, nor ear heard,
neither have entered into the heart of man, the things
which God hath prepared for them that love him.*
1 Corinthians 2:9

This very body of ours—who shall tell what it shall be like?
That it shall be transformed and made like unto the glorious
body of Christ Jesus our Lord we know. We may patiently
endure the cross, since we shall so soon receive the crown;
we may placidly go down to the grave, since we shall so tri-
umphantly come up from it; we may cheerfully take leave of
our lodgings here, since we have a home in prospect where
our kindred shall all be gathered, and our Sire never absent.

Brethren, we are, as it were, in a ship at sea today, tossed
with tempest—but we are to be in a palace ere long. You
observe how the figure changes, never tossed again, never
again put forth on a tempestuous sea. Like buildings and
mansions, we shall be fixed and permanent. In that land of
our inheritance is a freehold with its foundation of sapphire,
with its windows of agate, with its gates of carbuncle. What
a sweet surprise for the sons of poverty on earth!

Those jewels, since jewels are always connected with rank
or royalty, are meant to betoken the honors in the next world
to those who are humble and faithful in their sacred calling
here. You shall have such palaces as Oriental extravagance

could never emulate. Does it belong to kings to dwell in palaces? You shall be kings and priests unto God. A few more days of languishing, with their faint hopes and fretting fears, their throbbing temples and feverish pulse, ere Christ does bids you come. The Master calls for you. You must obey the summons. And what next? Forever with the Lord.

God has said it, and He will do it. Believe and rejoice therein therefore, for it is no fiction but a fact. Yet a little while and you shall leave your cottage for a mansion, your toil shall be exchanged for rest, your dishonor for glory, your pain for infinite pleasure. You shall find new company and better in yonder world of light. Though you close your eyes on fair prospects below, fairer scenes await you above. Be comforted!

"Sanctified Sorrow," Metropolitan Tabernacle Pulpit, No. 3435 (Undated)

GOD IS BIG WHEN OUR FAITH IS SMALL

For who hath despised the day of small things?
ZECHARIAH 4:10

Beware, my dear Christian friends, of living by feeling. He that lives by feelings will be happy today and unhappy tomorrow—and if our salvation depended upon our feelings, we should be lost one day and saved another, for they are as fickle as the weather and go up and down like a barometer. We live by faith, and if that faith be weak, bless God that weak faith is faith and that weak faith is true faith.

If you believe in Christ Jesus, though your faith be as a grain of mustard seed, it will save you—and it will, by and by, grow into something stronger. A diamond is a diamond, and the smallest scrap of it is of the same nature as the Koh-i-Noor, and he that has but little faith has faith for all that. And it is not great faith that is essential to salvation, but faith that links the soul to Christ—and that soul is, therefore, saved.

I think I hear you also add to all this the complaint that your other graces seem to be small too. "Oh," you say, "my patience is so little. If I have a little pain, I begin to cry out. I was in hopes I should be able to bear it—bear it without murmuring. My courage is so little—the blush is on my cheek if anybody asks me about Christ—I think I could hardly confess Him before half a dozen, much less before the world. I am very weak indeed."

Ah! I don't wonder. I have known some who have been strong by reason of years and have still been lacking in that virtue. But where faith is weak, of course, the rest will be weak. A plant that has a weak root will naturally have a weak stem and then will have but weak fruit. Your weakness of faith sends a weakness through the whole. But for all this, though you are to seek for more faith and consequently for more grace—for stronger graces, yet do not despise what graces you have. Thank God for them. And pray that the few clusters that are now upon you may be multiplied a thousandfold to the praise of the glory of His grace.

"Encouragement for the Depressed,"
Metropolitan Tabernacle Pulpit, No. 3489 (1871)

ANGUISHED PRAYER

And being in an agony he prayed more earnestly:
and his sweat was as it were great drops of
blood falling down to the ground.
LUKE 22:44

[Jesus] sought help in human companionship, and it was very natural that He should do so. God has created in our human nature a craving for sympathy. We do not err when we expect our brethren to watch with us in our hour of trial. But our Lord did not find that men were able to assist Him—however willing their spirit might be, their flesh was weak. What, then, did He do? He resorted to prayer, and especially prayer to God under the character of Father. I have learned by experience that we never know the sweetness of the Fatherhood of God so much as when we are in very bitter anguish. I can understand why the Savior said, "Abba, Father"—it was anguish that brought Him down as a chastened child to appeal plaintively to a Father's love. In the bitterness of my soul I have cried, "If, indeed, You are my Father, by the heart of Your Fatherhood have pity on Your child." And here Jesus pleads with His Father as we have done, and He finds comfort in that pleading.

Prayer was the channel of the Redeemer's comfort—earnest, intense, reverent, repeated prayer—and after each time of prayer, He seems to have grown quiet and to have gone to His disciples with a measure of restored peace of mind. The sight of their sleeping helped to bring back His griefs and, therefore, He returned to pray again. And each time He was comforted, so that when He had prayed for the third time, He was prepared to meet Judas and the soldiers and to go with silent patience to judgment and to death! His great comfort was prayer and submission to the divine will, for when He had laid His own will down at His Father's feet, the feebleness of His flesh spoke no more complainingly—but in sweet silence, like a sheep dumb before her shearers, He contained His soul in patience and rest.

Dear brothers and sisters, if any of you shall have your Gethsemane and your heavy griefs, imitate your Master by resorting to prayer, by crying to your Father, and by learning submission to His will.

"THE AGONY IN GETHSEMANE," METROPOLITAN TABERNACLE PULPIT, No. 1199 (1874)

NOBODY'S STRONGER THAN GOD

I will not fail thee, nor forsake thee.
JOSHUA 1:5

A sense of his own weakness comes over a man all the more from being associated with a grander mind. If you mingle with your inferiors, you are apt to grow vain—but closely associated with superior minds, there is a far greater probability that you will become depressed and may think even less of yourself than humility might require—for humility is, after all, only a right estimate of our own powers. Joshua, therefore, may possibly have been somewhat despondent under a very pressing sense of his own deficiencies; and this cheering assurance would meet his case—"I will not fail you: though you are less wise, or meek, or courageous than Moses, I will not fail you, nor forsake you."

If God is with our weakness, it waxes strong. If He is with our folly, it rises into wisdom. If He is with our timidity, it gathers courage. It matters not how conscious a man may be of being nothing at all in himself, when he is conscious of the divine presence, he even rejoices in his infirmity because the power of God rests upon him.

The consolation given to Joshua would be exceedingly suitable in the presence of his enemies. The other spies had said that these Canaanites dwelt in cities that were walled up to heaven, and though Joshua did not endorse that exaggeration, he was very well aware that the cities to be captured were fortresses of great strength. And he knew the people to be exterminated were men of ferocious courage and great physical energy. Therefore, the Lord said, "I will not fail you, nor forsake you." What more was needed? Surely, in the presence of God, Anakim become dwarfs, strongholds become as a lodge in a garden of cucumbers, and chariots of iron are as thistledown upon the hillside driven before the blast!

What is strong against the Most High? What is formidable in opposition to Jehovah? "If God is for us, who can be against us?" They that are with us are more than they that are against us, when once the Lord of Hosts is seen in our ranks! "Therefore will we not fear, though the earth be removed, the mountains be carried into the midst of the sea."

"Strengthening Medicine for God's Servants," Metropolitan Tabernacle Pulpit, No. 1214 (Undated)

THE PEACE OF GOD

And the peace of God, which passeth all understanding,
shall keep your hearts and minds through Christ Jesus.
Philippians 4:7

The man who believes in Jesus and is reconciled to God has nothing outside of him that he needs to fear. Is he poor? He rejoices that Christ makes poor men rich. Does he prosper? He rejoices that there is grace to sanctify his prosperity lest it become intoxicating to him. Does there lie before him a great trouble? He thanks God for His promise that as his day his strength shall be. Does he apprehend the loss of friends? He prays that the trial may be averted, for he is permitted so to pray, even as David begged for the life of his child. But, having so done, he feels sure that God will not take away an earthly friend unless it is with kind intent to gather up our trust and confidence more fully to Himself. Does there lie before him the prospect of speedy death? The hope of resurrection gives peace to his dying pillow. He knows that his Redeemer lives and he is content to let his body sleep in the dust awhile. Is he reminded by scripture of a day of judgment when all hearts shall be revealed? He has peace with regard to that dread mystery and all that surrounds it, for he knows whom he has believed and he knows that He will protect him in that day.

Whatever may be suggested that might alarm or distress

the believer, deep down in his soul he cannot be disturbed because he sees his God at the helm of the vessel holding the rudder with a hand which defies the storm. This is peculiarly advantageous in days like these when all things wear a dreary aspect. The storm signals are flying, the clouds are gathering, flashes of lightning and sounds of distant thunder are all around us.

Brethren, it is for the believer, in such a case, to feel no dismay, for our God is in the heavens and He does not forsake the throne. His purposes will be fulfilled and good will come out of evil, for at this very moment God sits in the council chambers of kings and orders all things according to the counsel of His will.

"THE PEACE OF GOD," METROPOLITAN
TABERNACLE PULPIT, NO. 1397 (1878)

FREE AT LAST

And he was teaching in one of the synagogues on the sabbath. And, behold, there was a woman which had a spirit of infirmity eighteen years, and was bowed together, and could in no wise lift up herself. And when Jesus saw her, he called her to him, and said unto her, Woman, thou art loosed from thine infirmity. And he laid his hands on her: and immediately she was made straight, and glorified God.
LUKE 13:10–13

Can a child of God be eighteen years in despondency? I am bound to answer, "Yes." Individuals have been locked up for many years in the gloomy den of despair and yet after all have been singularly brought out into joy and comfort.

Eighteen years' despondency must be a frightful affliction, and yet there is an escape out of it—for though the devil may take eighteen years to forge a chain, it does not take our blessed Lord eighteen minutes to break it. He can soon set the captive free. Build, build your dungeons, O Fiend of Hell, and lay the foundations deep and place the courses of granite so fast together that none can stir a stone of your fabric—but when *He* comes, your Master who will destroy all your works, *He* does but speak, and like the unsubstantial fabric of a vision your Bastille vanishes into thin air. Eighteen years of melancholy do not prove that Jesus cannot set the captive free; they only offer Him an opportunity for displaying His gracious power.

Note further about this poor woman that, bowed down as she was both in mind and body, she yet frequented the house of prayer. She might very well have said, "It is very painful for me to go into a public place, I ought to be excused." But no, there she was. Dear child of God, the devil has sometimes suggested to you that it is vain for you to go anymore to hear the Word. Go all the same. He knows you are likely to escape from his hands so long as you hear the Word, and therefore if he can keep you away he will do so. It was while in the house of prayer that this woman found her liberty—and there you may find it. Therefore still continue to go up to the house of the Lord, come what may.

"The Lifting Up of the Bowed Down,"
Metropolitan Tabernacle Pulpit, No. 1426 (1878)

HOUNDED BY TEMPTATIONS

Therefore being justified by faith, we have peace
with God through our Lord Jesus Christ.
ROMANS 5:1

I feel certain that the text tells us that every justified man has peace with God—and if so, why is it that I hear poor souls crying, "I believe, but I do not enjoy peace"? I think I can tell you why it is. You make a mistake as to what this peace is. You say, "I am so dreadfully tempted. Sometimes I am drawn this way and sometimes the other and the devil never lets me alone." Listen. Did you ever read in the Bible that you were to have peace with the devil? Look at the text: "Therefore being justified by faith, we have peace with God." That is a very different thing from having peace with Satan.

If the devil were to let you alone and never tempt you, I should begin to think that you belonged to him—for he is kind to his own in his own way for a while. He has a way of whispering soft things into their ears and then with dulcet notes and siren songs he lures them to eternal destruction. But he worries with a malicious joy those whom he cannot destroy, for in their case he has great wrath, knowing that his time is short. He expects to see you soon in heaven, out of gunshot of him—and so he makes the best of his opportunities to try, if he can, to distress and injure you while you are here. You will soon be so far above him that you will not be able to hear the hell-dog bark, and so he snaps at you now to see if he can hurt you, as once he did your Master when he wounded His heel.

You never had a promise of being at peace with the prince of darkness, but there is another promise which is far better. It is this: "The Lord shall bruise Satan under your feet shortly." A bruise it shall be when we have him under our feet—we will triumph like our Master in the breaking of his head. Till then, depend upon it, the enmity between the seed of the serpent and the seed of the woman will continue and there will be no truce to the war.

"Peace—A Fact and a Feeling," Metropolitan Tabernacle Pulpit, No. 1456 (1879)

LIGHT IN THE SHADOW

Yea, though I walk through the valley of the shadow of death, I will fear no evil: for thou art with me; thy rod and thy staff they comfort me.
PSALM 23:4

A man can pluck up courage against a thing he knows, but an evil which he does not know unmans him! He does not know what the trial is and yet a strange, joy-killing feeling is upon him. He cannot see the extent of his loss in business, but he fears that his all will go—he does not know the end of his child's illness, but death appears to be threatening. All is suspense and surmise and the evil of evils is uncertainty. That which frightened Belshazzar when the handwriting was on the wall was, no doubt, that he could see the hand but he could not see the arm and the body to which the hand belonged. So, sometimes, it seems to us as if we could not make out our condition—could not understand God's dealings with us. We have seemed to be at cross-purposes with providence. We have come to a place where two seas meet and we cannot understand the current. Our temptation has been comparable to a cyclone and we do not know which way the hurricane is sweeping—we are in the power of a whirlwind, jerked to and fro.

Such things happen to God's people now and then. And what are they to do when they get into these perplexities, these mysterious troubles that they cannot at all describe? They must do—and God help them to do—as this blessed man did, who in the peace and confidence of faith went on his way singing: Yea, though I walk through the valley shaded by the mysterious wings of death and though I know nothing of my way and cannot understand it, yet will I fear no evil, for You are with me. You know the way that I take. There are no mysteries with my God. You have the thread of this labyrinth and You will surely lead me through. Why, therefore, should I fear? Your rod and Your staff, they comfort me! Gloom, danger, mystery—these three all vanish when faith lights up her heavenly lamp, trimmed with the golden oil of the promise.

"THE VALLEY OF THE SHADOW OF DEATH,"
METROPOLITAN TABERNACLE PULPIT, NO. 1595 (1880)

JESUS UNDERSTANDS

For we have not an high priest which cannot be touched with the feeling of our infirmities; but was in all points tempted like as we are, yet without sin.
HEBREWS 4:15

It is surely true that a great number of God's best servants have trod the deeps of the Valley of the Shadow—and this ought to comfort some of you. The footsteps of the holy are in the Valley of Weeping. Saints have marched through the Via Dolorosa—do you not see their footprints? Above all others mark one footstep! Do you not see it? Stoop down and fix your gaze upon it! Go on your knees and view it! If you watch it well, you will observe the print of a nail. As surely as this Word of God is true, your Lord has felt the chill of the death-shade. There is no gloom of spirit, apart from the sin of it, into which Jesus has not fallen! There is no trouble of soul or turmoil of heart which is free from sin, which the Lord has not known. He says, "Reproach has broken My heart and I am full of heaviness." The footprint of the Lord of life is set in the rock forever, even in the valley of the shadow of death! Shall we not cheerfully advance to the cross and death of Jerusalem when Jesus goes before us?

No sin is necessarily connected with sorrow of heart, for Jesus Christ our Lord once said, "My soul is exceedingly sorrowful even unto death." There was no sin in Him, and consequently, none in His deep depression! We have never known a joy or a sorrow altogether untainted with evil, but in grief itself there is no necessary cause of sin. A man may be as happy as all the birds in the air and there may be no sin in his happiness. And a man may be exceedingly heavy and yet there may be no sin in the heaviness. I do not say that there is not sin in all our feelings but, still, the feelings in themselves need not be sinful! I would, therefore, try to cheer any brothers and sisters who are sad, for their sadness is not necessarily blameworthy.

"THE VALLEY OF THE SHADOW OF DEATH,"
METROPOLITAN TABERNACLE PULPIT, No. 1595 (1880)

NOTHING TO FEAR

Be strong and of a good courage, fear not, nor be afraid
of them: for the LORD thy God, he it is that doth go
with thee; he will not fail thee, nor forsake thee.
DEUTERONOMY 31:6

Have you, my friend, trouble evidently drawing near to you?
Are there tokens of a storm all around you? Then look bravely
at the future! Let not your heart fail you while waiting for
the thunder and the hurricane. David said, "Though a host
should encamp against me, my heart shall not fear; though
war should rise against me, in this will I be confident."
Encamped enemies generally trouble us more than actually
contending foes. When once the enemy raises the war cry
and comes on, we are awakened to valor and meet him,
foot to foot. But while he tarries and holds us in suspense,
our heart is apt to eat into itself with perplexity. We do not
know when his onslaught will be—this suspense distresses
the soul and, therefore, the glory of a faith that can say,
"Though I know that I shall soon suffer, yet in the prospect
of it I am at rest. I fear no evil." Beloved, pray to be calm in
the prospect of trial—it is half the battle! Is it not written
of the believer, "He shall not be afraid of evil tidings: his
heart is fixed, trusting in the Lord"?

We are generally in a hurry to get our trouble over, like
those who say, "If medicine must be taken, let it be taken as

61

soon as possible." There is a season for all things. Let us wait till the trouble comes from the hand of the Lord, for He will time it to the second. "There! I must know the worst of it," cries one. "I feel in such a horrible state of suspense that I must end it one way or another." But, my dear friend, faith is not in such a frightful bustle: "He that believes shall not make haste." Faith is quick when it has to serve God, but it is patient when it has to wait for Him. There is no hurry about the psalmist: "Yea, though I walk," he says—quietly, calmly, steadily. The pace of the experienced man of God is a walk.

"THE VALLEY OF THE SHADOW OF DEATH,"
METROPOLITAN TABERNACLE PULPIT, No. 1595 (1880)

WHEN STORMS RAGE

And he arose, and rebuked the wind, and said
unto the sea, Peace, be still. And the wind
ceased, and there was a great calm.
MARK 4:39

I have read of a little boy who was on board a vessel that was being buffeted by the tempest and everybody was distressed, knowing that the ship was in great peril. There was not a sailor on board, and certainly not a passenger, who was not full of fear. This boy, however, was perfectly happy and was rather amused than alarmed by the tossing of the ship. They asked him why he was so happy at such a time. "Well," he said, "my father is the captain. He knows how to manage." He did not think it possible that the ship could go down while his father was in command! There was folly in such confidence, but there will be none in yours if you believe with an equally unqualified faith in your Father who can and will bring safely into port every vessel that is committed to His charge! Rest in God and be quiet from fear of evil!

Was there ever a better reason given under heaven for being fearless than this, that God is with us? He is on our side! He is pledged to help us! He has never failed us. He must cease to be what He is before He can cast away one soul that trusts Him. Where, then, is there room for terror?

The child is confident because his mother is with

him—much more should we be serene in heart since the omniscient, the omnipotent, the immutable God is on our side! "Whom shall I fear?" Whom shall we select to honor with our dread? Is there anybody that we need to fear? "Who shall lay anything to the charge of God's elect? It is God that justifies. Who is he that condemns?" Christ has died and risen again and sits up yonder at the right hand of God as our representative—who, then, can harm us? Let the heavens be dissolved and the earth be melted with fervent heat, but let not the Christian's heart be moved! Let him stand like the great mountains whose foundations are confirmed forever, for the Lord God will not forsake His people or break His covenant. "I will fear no evil, for You are with me."

"THE VALLEY OF THE SHADOW OF DEATH,"
METROPOLITAN TABERNACLE PULPIT, NO. 1595 (1880)

PERSONAL AFFLICTIONS

For ever, O Lord, thy word is settled in heaven.
Thy faithfulness is unto all generations: thou hast
established the earth, and it abideth. They continue
this day according to thine ordinances: for all are
thy servants. Unless thy law had been my delights,
I should then have perished in mine affliction.
Psalm 119:89–92

Even in those psalms which are not associated with any particular chapter of history, we can often trace out the trail of the writer's experience and track his soul through its wanderings. His reflections then become vivid with intense reality. The meditation now before us is evidently prompted by some event deeply carved on the writer's memory.

"Unless Your law had been my delights, I should then have perished in my affliction." We know nothing of the time or circumstance when the heart was terrified, when the nerves were shaken, when the weakness of nature asserted itself. Possibly his affliction was long, but certainly it reached a crisis so perilous that his life then trembled in the balance. He was then ripe for destruction, ready to have perished. Moreover, it is noteworthy that whatever his trial may have been, whether it was a sickness or a disaster or any other manner of adversity, he refers to it as his own and he calls it "my affliction." At the sound of such words a stranger might well be touched with pity, but a friend, however sympathizing, would shrink from prying into the secrets of a heart that so delicately conceals its own bitterness.

The one and only thing that the psalmist was eager to tell us was the prescription that soothed his pains and sustained his spirits. On mature reflection he is confident that he would have perished under that affliction if it had not been for certain comfortable and delightful reflections concerning God's Word. There are plenty of miry places on the way to heaven and so it will be our wisdom to diligently inquire how this good man passed through them. I like to hear how any godly man has been comforted, for it comforts me. I take a deep interest in the simple tale of any humble prisoner whose bonds the Lord has loosed. And I feel it a choice pleasure to chime in with songs of thanksgiving which come from the lips of grateful suppliants whose cries the Lord has heard.

"My Solace in My Affliction," Metropolitan Tabernacle Pulpit, No. 1656 (1882)

A STEADYING HAND

Who laid the foundations of the earth,
that it should not be removed for ever.
PSALM 104:5

Look at the earth. We talk of the pillars of it—the columns
upon which it leans—but what does it rest upon? The earth
rests upon nothing. There it is floating in space, and yet it has
never drifted from its place or turned aside from its proper
orbit. There are little quivers within its own bosom, but it
does not rush away from the place where God ordained it
to be. It continues its course around the sun with immutable
fidelity. This world is rather larger than you are, and requires
more power to keep it in its place than is requisite to keep you
in your place. Yet there it is. Shall not the Lord hold up His
servant and keep him from wandering? All the machinery in
the world could not turn the globe on its axis or move it in
its orbit. I suppose that no angelic force would be adequate
to bring about such results as God accomplishes simply by
His will. He establishes the world and it abides.

Nor, brethren, is it this world alone, vast though it may
seem to us, yet a little planet amidst the larger spheres. The
Lord upholds all worlds comprehended in one vast system.
"They continue this day according to Your ordinances."
Every star maintains its place. "One sun by day, by night
ten thousand shine," yet these constellations, and all other

creations of God's hand, observe each one the ordinance of heaven. God does not swerve from His own statutes, nor does He suffer the shining hosts to break their ranks. They may not rush about in wild confusion; they are the sentinels of heaven. He calls them all by name as He musters and marshals their serried ranks. Are they not all His servants, waiting at His feet as maidens attend their mistress? They all do His bidding. Ought not this cheer our hearts and inspire us with courage? If the heavenly bodies—as we are known to call those inanimate creatures of the Most High—are upheld by His power and disposed of by His wisdom, why should we discredit the omnipotence which preserves our souls, or the omniscience which orders our steps?

"MY SOLACE IN MY AFFLICTION," METROPOLITAN TABERNACLE PULPIT, NO. 1656 (1882)

68

WHEN OUR HEARTBREAK MEETS HIS FAITHFULNESS

*Withhold not thou thy tender mercies from
me, O LORD: let thy lovingkindness and
thy truth continually preserve me.*

PSALM 40:11

It is in such seasons of acute distress, when this world has
no soothing to offer, that God's Word can minister infinite
delights to soothe the distractions and heal the sorrows of
the heart. These psalms—most of them written by David, and
the rest written by disciples of the David school—compass
almost every conceivable form of adversity that our poor
suffering humanity is exposed. And there is another thing
which I am sure you will find it sweet to muse upon. It is
this: in all cases the sigh was turned into a song before it
was admitted into the sacred calendar. This is a law of the
kingdom of heaven over which I linger with unspeakable
delight. In fact, I can take a survey of your troubles, as well
as of my own, with much composure when I perceive that
they are all capable of being turned into joy.

Our sympathies are continually stirred by the bereave-
ments one and another of us are called to suffer. The ties of
kindred and friendship are being broken all around. Each
day has its obituary. This goes on from generation to generation. But the sharp pang of losing those we love is in no

wise lightened by the fact that it is so general. Some of us today live in dread; others have drawn down the blinds. I hear your desolate moan, but there is music not far off. All creatures are shadows, yet there is substance.

At length you turn to these scriptures, and as you read, "The Lord lives; and blessed be my Rock; and exalted be the God of the rock of my salvation," your soul revives. You quit the treacherous sea and reach the solid rock, when you repeat the words, "Lord, You have been our dwelling place in all generations." Alas, dear mourner, your thoughts have wandered like the dove from out the ark, over the watery waste, but now again Noah's hand encloses you. There you have calm and peaceful rest. Here is the pillow on which your aching head can lie at ease: "You are the same; of Your years there is no end." Such delights can sustain a sinking soul.

"My Solace in My Affliction," Metropolitan
Tabernacle Pulpit, No. 1656 (1882)

PRESENT SADNESS YIELDS ETERNAL GLADNESS

Make us glad according to the days wherein thou hast afflicted us, and the years wherein we have seen evil.
PSALM 90:15

In the spiritual life God does not run us up with glittering virtues all of a sudden, but deep prostration of spirit and thorough humiliation prepare the under-courses. And then, afterwards, stone upon stone, as with rows of jewels, we are built up to be a palace for the indwelling of God. Sorrow furnishes the house for joy. The preparation for an eternal heaven is temporary affliction. Jesus has gone to prepare heaven for us, but He has left His cross behind Him that the Holy Spirit may by its means prepare us for heaven. You could not enjoy the rest of paradise if you had not first known the labors of pilgrimage. You could not understand the boundless felicity of heaven if your hearts had not been enlarged by the endurance of tribulation. Let not this be forgotten, then—that our troubles build a house and spread a table for our joys.

Did you ever read of a Roman triumph? Have you ever stood upon the Via Sacra which led up to the Capitol? There, when the glad day was come, the people crowded all along the road. Every house-roof was loaded, the very chimney tops bore each a man, while along the sacred way the conqueror rode, drawn by white horses, amid the blast of trumpets and the thundering acclamations of myriads. What glory! What renown! Rome's millions did their best to crown their hero.

But there had been to him full many a battle before that hour of pride. Victory needs conflict as its preface. The conqueror's scars are his truest decorations; his wounds are his best certificates of valor. Because he had been smothered with the dust and defiled with the blood of battle, therefore the hero stood erect and all men paid him reverence. It must be so in the present condition of things. No man can wear the garland till he has first contended for it. "Sure we must fight if we would reign. Increase our courage, Lord!" The way to the crown is by the cross; the palm branch comes not to the idle hand.

"GLADNESS FOR SADNESS," METROPOLITAN
TABERNACLE PULPIT, NO. 1701 (1883)

JOY AWAITS

Let thy work appear unto thy servants,
and thy glory unto their children.
PSALM 90:16

The departed possess a joy which outweighs your mourning. It is a great sorrow to lose a father, but it is a greater joy to know that your father is not really lost, but translated to the skies. It is a great grief to part with a true brother and fellow laborer, but it is happiness to know that he is promoted to the peerage of the skies. We might each one say of our departed friend, "Let us go, that we may die with him." These good men have the start of us, they are preferred before us, they have first seen the King in His beauty. We have more in heaven to love, more fraternal meetings to anticipate, and so we have new links with the eternal. Said I not truly, that every sorrow contains a joy?

Once more, the day will come when all the sorrows of God's sending will be looked upon as joys. Hear you this! By some strange alchemy, known only to "the King eternal, immortal, invisible," our sorrows shall be turned into joys. You see this in your own homes—I quote it because it is the Lord's own metaphor—a woman when she is in travail has sorrow because her hour is come. But soon she remembers no more her travail, for joy that a man is born into the world.

Before we enter heaven we shall thank God for most of

our sorrow, and when we are once in glory we shall thank Him for it all. Perhaps in heaven, among all the things which have happened to us, that will excite our wonder and delight, our furnace experience and the hammer and the file will take the lead. Sorrow will contribute rich stanzas to our everlasting psalm. Wherefore comfort one another with these words, and breathe the prayer each one today: "Make us glad according to the days wherein You have afflicted us, and the years wherein we have seen evil." In each case may divine love weigh out the ingredients of a sanctified life according to the art of the apothecary, each one in due proportion.

"GLADNESS FOR SADNESS," METROPOLITAN
TABERNACLE PULPIT, No. 1701 (1883)

FAITH TRUMPS ANXIETY

And he said unto them, Why are ye so
fearful? how is it that ye have no faith?
MARK 4:40

─────────────

Our Lord questioned His apostles thus, not only because their unbelief grieved Him but because it was most unreasonable. The most unreasonable thing in the world is to doubt God. Faith is pure reason. That may seem a strange paradox, but it is literally true; nothing is so reasonable as to believe the word of God, who cannot err or lie.

The fears of the tempest-tossed disciples were unreasonable because they were contrary to their own belief. They did believe that Jesus was sent of God upon a glorious mission—how could that mission be accomplished if He was drowned? If they sank in the sea, He must sink, too, for they were embarked in the same boat. Ought not the faith they had in His divine mission to have kept them hopeful even in the worst moment of the storm? My brethren, be not inconsistent with what you do believe. Do not deny your own creed, however slender it may be, for that is irrational.

Moreover, their fears were opposed to their own experience; they had seen their Lord work miracles, and miracles for them too. They had already beheld abundant proofs of His power and godhead and of His care on their behalf. Is not this true of us also? Has the Lord ever failed us? Has

He not helped us to this day? Are you going to fly in the teeth of all your past experience? Is all that you have ever believed of God a fiction? Have you been under a gross delusion up to this day?

Their fears were altogether inconsistent with their observation. They had seen Jesus heal the sick and feed the multitudes. I am not quite sure how many of His miracles had already been worked before them, but certainly enough for their observation to compel them to believe that He was able to save them from death. How, then, could they doubt? But have not we also seen enough of the finger of God to be confident in the day of trouble? If we believe not, we dare not lay the blame upon the lack of evidence. To mistrust is irrational, because it is contrary to all the experience of our hearts, and the observation of our eyes.

"WHY IS FAITH SO FEEBLE?" METROPOLITAN TABERNACLE PULPIT, No. 1964 (1887)

THE DISCIPLES' MISPLACED TRUST

*And there arose a great storm of wind, and the
waves beat into the ship, so that it was now full.
And he was in the hinder part of the ship, asleep
on a pillow: and they awake him, and say unto
him, Master, carest thou not that we perish?*
MARK 4:37–38

The inquiry as to why we are so fearful may be helped by
another question: Is it that our trials take us by surprise?
Perhaps the disciples reckoned that everything must be right
since they had Christ on board. Let us not indulge such a
notion. Never let any affliction surprise you, for your Lord
has told you, "In the world you shall have tribulation." If your
children die, do not be surprised; shall mortal parents bring
forth immortal offspring? If your riches disappear, do not
be surprised. They always had wings—what wonder if they
fly! If any other adversity happens to you, be not surprised,
for "man is born unto trouble, as the sparks fly upward." The
Lord has told you before it come to pass, that when it is
come to pass you may believe. Reckon upon tribulation, and
then you will not be overtaken by surprise, or fret as though
some strange thing had happened to you.

Why were they so full of fear? Was it lack of simplicity
of confidence? Did they trust in their good boat or feel that

they were safe because of their seamanship? Brethren, we are never as weak as when we feel strongest and never so foolish as when we dream that we are wise. When you are "up to the mark," you will soon be down to the mark. When our confidence is partly in God and partly in ourselves, our overthrow is not far off. That angel, who stood with one foot upon the sea and the other upon the earth, would have been drowned if he had not been an angel. As you are not an angel, take care that you put both feet upon the *terra firma* of divine strength and truth. If you trust in yourself in the least degree, one link of the chain is too weak to bear you—and it is of no avail that the other links are strong.

"WHY IS FAITH SO FEEBLE?" METROPOLITAN
TABERNACLE PULPIT, NO. 1964 (1887)

GOD'S ASSURING MIRACLES

To him who alone doeth great wonders:
for his mercy endureth for ever.
PSALM 136:4

———————————————

[God] acts according to His nature when He does great wonders. He is so wonderful a God that no one has ever formed an adequate conception of Him. We do not understand God, nor can we comprehend Him. We know that there is such a one and we love and praise Him—but to say that we understand God, as a man is understood by his fellow, would be very far from the truth. Ten thousand minds, educated to the highest and even filled with the Holy Spirit, if they could unite their largest ideas could not compass the infinite Jehovah. You have filled so many little cups with the waters of the sea, but you are as far off as ever from having taken up the great deep. It is but natural that the Infinite One should do great wonders. Oh, that we would believe Him to be great, then should we with Mary sing, "My soul does magnify the Lord, and my spirit does rejoice in God my Savior."

Do not despondingly imagine that God will allow His wonders to dwindle down as the world grows old. Is that your God? My God is the same; He faints not, neither is weary. He still does great wonders. Jehovah who divided the Red Sea is our God forever and ever; He could divide the

Atlantic if He willed it, and would do so if it were needful for the fulfillment of His gracious purposes. The God who fed His people in the wilderness may not cause manna to fall from heaven today, but He will none the less give food unto His people. "Your place of defense shall be the munitions of rocks; your bread shall be given you, and your waters shall be sure."

The Lord can do as much today as He did in the elder ages; yes, we may look for greater things than these. I do not believe that God's music is now marked with *diminuendo*, but I see *crescendo* on the score. It grows in volume and in force as the ages roll along. The Lord leads our wondering minds on from height to height, and reveals to us more and more the glory of His power.

"God the Wonder-Worker," Metropolitan Tabernacle Pulpit, No. 1981 (1887)

THE SOURCE OF PEACE

These things I have spoken unto you,
that in me ye might have peace.
JOHN 16:33

It is worthy of careful consideration that in Jesus Himself there was ever present an abiding peace. He had peace. If He had not Himself possessed peace, we could not have had peace in Him. But what a holy calm there was upon the spirit of our divine Master!

When His eager and foolish disciples would push Him forward or would hold Him back, He was moved neither in the one direction nor in the other by any of them—but He steadfastly held to the even tenor of His way, His soul abiding in God, giving glory to God and resting in the eternal power and godhead which He knew to be always at His side. The background of the life of Christ is the omnipresence of the Father. Wherever you see Him—if you see Him quite alone when every disciple has forsaken Him—you see this text expounded, "You will leave me alone, and yet I am not alone, because the Father is with me."

Now this fact that He felt the presence of the Father and did not occasionally speak to God but dwelt with Him—that He did not resort to God as a makeshift in time of trouble but abode with God at all times, and so kept His spirit above everything that would draw it down—this it was that filled

Him with an unbroken peace. Even Gethsemane did not break that peace. Covered with the bloody sweat, He still cries, "Not as I will, but as you will."

O friends, Christ has peace enough and to spare. He is Himself, personally, the deep wellspring of an endless peace—and therefore we can understand why we always find peace in Him. One calm and quiet man has sometimes spread peace through what else would have been terrified company. One Paul standing in the sinking ship saves all from ruin by the majesty of his immovable courage, and one Christ—such a Christ as ours—in the midst of a church turns a horde of cowards into an army of heroes. His infinite peace breathes peace into our vacillating spirits. We rest because we see how He rests.

"SWEET PEACE FOR TRIED BELIEVERS," METROPOLITAN
TABERNACLE PULPIT, NO. 1994 (1887)

JESUS OVERCOMES OUR FEAR

In the world ye shall have tribulation: but be of good cheer; I have overcome the world.

JOHN 16:33

Now, here is a matter of joyful consideration; our Lord says, "Be of good cheer; I have overcome the world." But what cheer is there in that? Well, the cheer lies in the fact which He does not here state, but which He had stated before—namely, that He is one with us and we are one with Him. He does as good as say, "I have overcome the world, and you are in Me, your Head. My overcoming of the world belongs to you. I, your Leader, have overcome the world for you. I have led the way in this dread fight, and conquered the adversaries which you have now to fight with, and thus I have virtually won the battle before you begin it."

> *Hell and your sins obstruct thy course,*
> *But hell and sins are vanquished foes:*
> *Your Jesus nailed them to His cross,*
> *And sang the triumph when He rose.*

"I have Myself," says Jesus, "overcome for you that you may overcome in Me. Now, go to the fight to rout the already worsted enemy, and triumph over a serpent whose head I have already broken."

We derive, then, from the fact that Christ has overcome, the assurance that we shall overcome since we are one with Him—members of His body and parts of Himself. O brothers, sisters, you must fight your way through. You cannot quit this conflict.

A great commander commences a campaign. Does he desire that there shall be no battle? If so, how is it a war? How is he a soldier? He certainly can send home no reports of victory if there is no fighting. He can never come to be a great commander if he never distinguishes himself in the field. So let us consider that every battlefield to which God calls us is only another opportunity of victory and, Christ being with us, another certainty of victory. Onward, then, you Christian soldiers!

Let your drooping hearts be glad;
March in heavenly armor clad.

"Sweet Peace for Tried Believers," Metropolitan Tabernacle Pulpit, No. 1994 (1887)

ANXIOUS PRAYERS

Give ear, O LORD, unto my prayer; and attend to the
voice of my supplications. In the day of my trouble
I will call upon thee: for thou wilt answer me.
PSALM 86:6–7

Note one thing about this remarkable prayer of David—it
is almost entirely devoid of poetry. Men use grand, studied,
rapturous, and poetical expressions in their praises, and they
do well. Let God be praised with the noblest thoughts, as
well as the most charming music. But when a man comes to
prayer—and that prayer is out of the depths of sorrow—he
has no time or thought for poetry. He goes straight at the
matter in hand, and pleads with God in downright plainness
of speech.

You shall notice that in happy prayers, in times of joy,
men use similes and metaphors and tropes and symbols and
the like, but when it comes to wrestling with God in times
of agony, there is no beauty of speech—parable and prose are
laid aside. The man's language is in sackcloth and ashes or,
better still, it stands stripped for wrestling, every superfluous
word being laid aside. Then the cry is heard, "I will not let
thee go, except thou bless me." That is not poetry, but it is
a great deal better.

Men cannot study where to put their feet prettily when
they are wrestling—they have to do the best they can to hold

their ground and fling their antagonist. In such a prayer-psalm as this, there is no studying of language—it is the pouring out of the heart as the heart boils over, the utterance of the desires as they bubble up from the soul's deeps, with an entire carelessness as to the fashion of the expression.

This ought to be a hint to you when you pray. Do not study how to arrange your words when you come before the Lord. Leave the expression to the occasion; it shall be given you in the selfsame hour what you shall speak. When your heart is like a boiling geyser, let it steam aloft in pillars of prayer. The overflowing of the soul is the best praying in the world. Prayers that are indistinct, inharmonious, broken, made up of sighs and cries and damped with tears—these are the prayers which win with heaven.

"CONCERNING PRAYER," METROPOLITAN
TABERNACLE PULPIT, NO. 2053 (1888)

HE KNOWS OUR TEARS

Jesus wept.
JOHN 11:35

Jesus wept in full knowledge of several things which might have prevented His weeping. You have sometimes thought to yourself when weeping at the grave of a dear child or wife or husband that you have been wrong in so doing. But this may not be the case. Our Savior wept, though He knew that Lazarus was safe enough. And yet, "Jesus wept."

Moreover, Jesus knew that He was going to raise Lazarus to life—his resurrection was close at hand. And yet, "Jesus wept." Sometimes we are told that if we really believed that our friends would rise again and that they are safe and happy even now, we would not weep. Why not? Jesus did. There cannot be any error in following where Jesus leads the way. Jesus knew, moreover, that the death of Lazarus was for the glory of God—He had said, "This sickness is not unto death but for the glory of God." And yet He wept! Have we not thought, "Surely it must be wicked to weep when you know that the bereavement will glorify God"? Not so, or else Jesus would not have wept under similar circumstances. Learn instruction—tears which else we might have regarded as contraband have now free admission into the realm of holiness, since "Jesus wept." You may weep, for Jesus wept. He wept, with full knowledge of the happiness of Lazarus, with full expectation of his resurrection and with the firm assurance that God was glorified even by his death—we may not, therefore, condemn what Christ allows.

"Jesus wept," but He did not sin. There was not even a particle of evil in any one of the Redeemer's tears. It is not a sin to weep for those whom God has taken away from us, nor for those who are suffering. I will tell you why there was no sin in Christ's weeping—it was because He wept in His Father's presence. When He spoke in His sorrow, the first word was *Father*. He said, "Father, I thank You." If you can weep in such a way that all the while you feel God to be your Father and can thank Him and know that you are in His presence, your weeping is not blameworthy but healthful. Let such floods flow on, for Jesus wept and said, "Father, I thank You."

"JESUS WEPT," METROPOLITAN TABERNACLE
PULPIT, No. 2091 (1889)

ANXIETY-ERASING PEACE

And, having made peace through the blood of his cross,
by him to reconcile all things unto himself; by him, I say,
whether they be things in earth, or things in heaven.
COLOSSIANS 1:20

God alone can speak true peace to the soul. When once a soul begins to feel its sinfulness and to tremble at the wrath to come, none but God can speak peace to it. Ministers cannot. I have often failed, when I have desired to bring comfort to troubled hearts. Books cannot do it, not even the most wise and gracious of them. The Bible itself cannot do it, apart from the Spirit of God. The ordinances of God's house, whether they are baptism or the Lord's Supper or prayer or preaching—none of these can bring peace to a heart apart from the still, small voice of the Lord! I pray that none of you may rest in anything short of a divine assurance of salvation. See how the waves are tossing themselves on high! Hark to the howling of the wind! Rise, Peter, and bid the waves be quiet! Awake, John, and pour oil upon the waves! Ah, sirs, the apostles will themselves sink unless a greater than they shall interpose. Only He who lay asleep near the tiller could say, "Peace, be still!" May He say that to everyone here who is troubled about his sins!

One word from the Lord is the quietus of all trouble. No deed is needed, only a word! The Lord Jesus, who is our peace, went up to the tree bearing our iniquities and thus removed the dread cause of the great warfare between God and man; there He ended the quarrel of the covenant. Listen to these words: "The chastisement of our peace was upon him." He made peace by the blood of His cross. Through His death, being justified by faith, we have peace with God: "It is finished." Righteousness and peace have kissed each other. Now is the way paved for man to come back to God by reconciliation through sacrifice; there is no more blood to be shed, nor sacrifice to be offered. Peace is finally made, and it only remains for the Lord God to speak it to the conscience and heart by the Holy Spirit.

"PEACE—HOW GAINED, HOW BROKEN," METROPOLITAN
TABERNACLE PULPIT, NO. 2112 (1889)

PROMISED PEACE

I will hear what God the Lord will speak:
for he will speak peace unto his people, and to his
saints: but let them not turn again to folly.
Psalm 85:8

Sooner or later the Lord will speak peace to His own. How blessed are the shalls and wills of the Lord God!—"He *will* speak peace unto his people." Doubt it not. He *will*. He *will*. Some of you have lost your peace for a while. Yet, if you are believers, "he will speak peace unto his people." You have come to Christ, and trust Him, but you do not enjoy such peace as you desire. "He will speak peace unto his people." There may be a time of battling and of struggling, the noise of war may disturb the camp for months but—in the end—"he will speak peace unto his people." I have seen some of the Lord's true people terribly harassed year after year. One for a very long time was in the dark, wrecked on a barbarous coast and neither sun nor moon appearing. But he was a true child of God, and at length he came out into the light and wrote a book which has cheered many.

If peace comes not before yet, "mark the perfect man and behold the upright: for the end of that man is peace." The Lord will not put His child to bed in the dark—He will light his candle before he sleeps the sleep of death. Sickness of body and weakness of mind, or some other cause, may be a terrible killjoy—but in the end, the Lord will speak peace unto His people. He cannot finally leave a soul that trusts in Him; no believer shall die of despair! You may sink very low—but underneath are the everlasting arms and these will bring you up again.

"PEACE—HOW GAINED, HOW BROKEN," METROPOLITAN TABERNACLE PULPIT, NO. 2112 (1889)

BETTER DAYS ARE COMING

As the tender grass springing out of the
earth by clear shining after rain.
2 Samuel 23:4

Times of gloom are to be expected. Oh, that wars might cease unto the ends of the earth! War is the sum of all villainies. There is nothing to be said for it. It is a monstrous thing that men should murder one another wholesale. But there will be no end of war from anything that you and I can do apart from preaching the gospel of Christ. When the King comes, when Jesus comes, when the King shall reign in righteousness, there will be an end to war—but till then there will be wars and rumors of wars, and when you hear of them, do not be disturbed as though everything was going to pieces. There will be clear shinings after the rain. Ay, though it be a reign of blood, afterwards He shall shine out who is our peace, and who will set up an unsuffering kingdom which shall know no end.

In religious matters, do not expect that the world will go on getting better and better. You may see, somebody will see, a falling away before the coming of Christ and a departure from the faith. "The love of many shall wax cold." It shall come to pass that, if you ask for faith, you will scarcely find it, for "when the Son of man cometh, shall he find faith on the earth?" Scarcely. It will be a very rare commodity, but be not distressed—even though all men are turned aside from the Christ of God for there will be clear shinings after the rain.

Although times of gloom are to be expected, an age of light will follow. There will come a day when Christ shall reign amongst His ancients gloriously, when the ungodly shall hide themselves in obscure places, the meek shall have dominion in the earth, and the sons of God in that morning shall be owned as the noblest of men. There is to come yet "a thousand years" (whatever that period may mean) of a reign of righteousness, wherein the whole of the earth shall be filled with the glory of God and become the vestibule of heaven. Have comfort about that glorious truth.

"CLEAR SHINING AFTER RAIN," METROPOLITAN
TABERNACLE PULPIT, No. 2284 (1890)

IMPATIENCE ONLY LEADS TO ANXIETY

When they therefore were come together, they asked
of him, saying, Lord, wilt thou at this time restore
again the kingdom to Israel? And he said unto them,
It is not for you to know the times or the seasons,
which the Father hath put in his own power.

ACTS 1:6–7

Possess your souls in patience—the things that are foretold are sure to happen. "Though the vision tarry, wait for it; because it will surely come, it will not tarry." I am persuaded that God never is before His time, but He never is too late. He never failed to keep tryst with His people to the tick of the clock. The future is in the Father's power.

And especially let it be remembered that it is in His power as our Father. He must arrange it rightly. He must arrange it in infinite love to us. It cannot be that, in some dark hour yet to come, He will forget us. He is our Father—will He forget His children? If the times could be in my hand, how earnestly would I pray that Christ would take them into His hand, or that the Father would take away from me the dangerous power and wield it all Himself! Did we not sing just now,

All my times are in Thy hand,
All events at Thy command?

The time of birth, the time of the new birth, the time of a sore trial, the time of the death of your beloved one, the time of your sickness and how long it shall last—all these times must come and last and end as shall please your Father. It is for you to know that your Father is at the helm of the ship and therefore it cannot be wrecked. It may rock and reel to and fro, but since He rules the waves, the vessel will not have one more tossing than His infinite love permits. Let us, then, not seek to unroll the map of the future, but calmly say,

> *My God, I would not long to see*
> *My fate with curious eyes,*
> *What gloomy lines are writ for me,*
> *Or what bright scenes arise.*

"WITNESSING BETTER THAN KNOWING THE FUTURE,"
METROPOLITAN TABERNACLE PULPIT, NO. 2330 (1889)

DON'T WORRY— YOU'RE NOT FORGOTTEN

I have formed thee; thou art my servant:
O Israel, thou shalt not be forgotten of me.
ISAIAH 44:21

What does this promise mean? It means first, that God will never cease to love His servants. If you are His servants, He loved you before the world began, He loves you still, and He will love you world without end.

Next, it means that the Lord will never cease to think of His servants. The thoughts of God are wonderful. He can think of every individual saint as much as if there were no other saint in the universe. He never leaves off thinking of each one of His people. The divine mind is distinctly set on you, brother—on you, sister—and it is never taken off from you. If God were to cease to think of us for five minutes, in that five minutes we might be ruined. But He never forgets us, and consequently, there shall be no part of our body without its armor and no portion of our time without a sentinel set to watch over us every single moment of it.

Next, the Lord will never cease to befriend His servants. God's thoughts are always practical; the gifts of His hands go with the thoughts of His mind. Our text means, "Thou shalt not be forgotten of Me in the distribution of My benefits." The Lord will not cease to give you bread and water and garments. His providence shall always take care of you.

I think I hear some dear child of God crying, "I was afraid that the Lord had forgotten me the other day." What right had you to think anything of the kind? Will the Lord cast off His people? Will He be faithful no more? The Lord says, "Thou shalt not be forgotten of me," and He will stand to it—depend upon it—and you shall share with the rest of His people in the high privileges of the covenant of His grace. He will not cease to love you, nor cease to think of you, nor cease to befriend and benefit you. With John Newton, you may sing,

> *His love in time past forbids me to think*
> *He'll leave me at last in trouble to sink;*
> *Each sweet Ebenezer I have in review,*
> *Confirms His good pleasure to help me quite through.*

"FORGET THEE, I WILL NOT," METROPOLITAN
TABERNACLE PULPIT, NO. 2384 (1888)

GOD STRENGTHENS ANXIOUS HEARTS

*Be of good courage, and he shall strengthen
your heart, all ye that hope in the LORD.*
PSALM 31:24

_____

God alone can strengthen the heart. How does God strengthen men's hearts? Well, sometimes by gracious providences. Something very unexpected happens. I have, myself, learned to expect the unexpected. I have known what it is almost to wish to get into a defile, through which there was no way of escape, that I might see the Lord cleave the hills asunder or divide even the sea to make a way for His people.

It is a grand thing to get into such deep water that you cannot touch the bottom and must swim—and then to feel the eternal buoyancy of God's providence bearing you up. It is grand swimming when there are ten thousand fathoms of ocean below you, there is no fear of knocking your foot against a rock then, and when you get right out into a simple dependence upon the living God and feel the waves of His eternal influences round about you, then will you be happy and blessed.

The Lord also has a way of strengthening men's hearts by the kindly fellowship of friends. Paul was often much refreshed by Christian associates. The Lord can send someone who, "as iron sharpeneth iron," may sharpen you and make you ready for service. So too have I known a man's heart to be mightily strengthened by a precious promise. Who knows the wonderful power of a text of scripture? What strength it gives to the loins! How we seem to be braced up when we truly lay hold of a promise of God, and it really gets a grip upon our spirit!

Beside all that, God the Holy Spirit has a secret way of strengthening the courage of God's people which none of us can explain. Have you ever felt it? You may have gone to your bed, sick at heart, "weary, and worn, and sad," and you wake in the morning ready for anything. Perhaps in the middle of the night you awake, and the visitations of God are manifested to you, and you feel as happy as if everything went the way you would like it to go. You feel a sudden strengthening of your spirit, so that you are perfectly resigned, satisfied, prepared, and ready.

"THE CURE FOR A WEAK HEART," METROPOLITAN TABERNACLE PULPIT, No. 2455 (1886)

JESUS HEALS WOUNDED SPIRITS

The spirit of a man will sustain his infirmity;
but a wounded spirit who can bear?
PROVERBS 18:14

One thing however, I would say to one who has a really wounded heart: Remember Christ's sympathy with you. O you who are tossed with tempest and not comforted, your Lord's vessel is in the storm with you! Yes, He is in the vessel with you. There is not a pang that rends the believer's heart but He has felt it first. He drinks out of the cup with you. Is it very bitter? He has had a cup full of it for every drop that you taste! This ought to comfort you. I know of no better remedy for the heart's trouble in a Christian than to feel, "My Master Himself takes no better portion than that which He gives to me."

Also let me recommend, as a choice remedy for a wounded spirit, an enlarged view of the love of God. I wish that some of you who have a wounded spirit would give God credit for being as kind as you are yourself. You would not suffer your child to endure a needless pain if you could remove it—neither does God afflict willingly or grieve the children of men. His delight is that you should be happy and joyful. Do not think that you may not take the comfort which He has set before you in His Word—He has put it there on purpose for you. Dare to take it, and think well of God, and it shall be well with your soul.

You are not the first child of God who has been depressed or troubled. Ay, among the noblest men and women who ever lived, there has been much of this kind of thing. Do not therefore think that you are quite alone in your sorrow. Bow your head and bear it, if it cannot be removed, for but a little while every cloud shall be swept away and you, in the cloudless sunlight, shall behold your God. Meanwhile, His strength is sufficient for you. He will not suffer you to be tempted above what you are able to bear, and if you cannot bear your infirmity because of your wounded spirit, He will bear for you both yourself and your infirmity.

"THE CAUSE AND CURE OF A WOUNDED SPIRIT,"
METROPOLITAN TABERNACLE PULPIT, No. 2494 (1885)

THE RESURRECTION—
A GRIEF-DEFEATING TRUTH

Now when Jesus was risen early the first day of the week,
he appeared first to Mary Magdalene, out of whom
he had cast seven devils. And she went and told them
that had been with him, as they mourned and wept.
MARK 16:9–10

So, I prefer to ask you to look at the consoling messenger who came to the disciples and said, concerning their Lord and ours, "He is not dead: he is risen." It is very important that we should have right views concerning the resurrection as well as the death of our Lord. If I go down my garden tomorrow morning early with my spirit drooping and disconsolate, and say to myself, "Alas! the world is in a very bad state and the church is almost as bad as the world. Everything is going wrong—everything is wretched, sad, and miserable," even the very birds might begin to say, "What is that man at? He is out of tune with us."

And if I look at the flowers, surely they also might well begin to chide me and say, "Master, what are you at?" But if I go forth, with many burdens and many cares all cast upon the Lord and with all the outlook, dreary as it is, still say, "The Lord liveth, and blessed be my rock, and let the God of my salvation be exalted," then surely the mountains and the hills shall break forth before me into singing and all the trees of the field shall clap their hands.

God means His people to rejoice, and the world, wilderness as it is, is to rejoice with them. "The wilderness and the solitary place shall be glad for them; and the desert shall rejoice, and blossom as the rose." God fill your souls with sunlight, all of you who are His people! If there is any truth that can flood our souls with joy, surely it is contained in the cheering message which Mary brought to the weeping disciples.

You and I, beloved, by our sins slew the Christ of God. He died the accursed death of the cross, but He is not dead. He is not dead now. That message of Mary Magdalene has changed the whole aspect of affairs, and though we have wept and mourned, now we will begin to rejoice.

"A Sad Interior and a Cheery Messenger,"
Metropolitan Tabernacle Pulpit, No. 2518 (1885)

OUR RELATABLE, SUFFERING SAVIOR

For Christ also hath once suffered for sins.
1 PETER 3:18

The apostle does not give us details of Christ's sufferings, but he lets us, for a moment, look into this condensation of them: "Christ also hath once suffered."

It is the epitome of His whole earthly existence up to the time of His rising from the dead. Christ begins His life here with suffering. He is born into the world, but there is "no room for him in the inn." He must lie in a manger, where the horned oxen feed. He is born of a poor mother; He must know the ills of poverty and, worse still, Herod seeks the young child's life. He must be hurried away by night into Egypt; He must be a stranger in a strange land, with His life in peril from a bloodthirsty tyrant.

When He comes back from Egypt, He grows in wisdom, and stature, and in favor with God and men. But you may rest assured that the years He spent in the carpenter's shop at Nazareth, though we are not told about them, were years of sore travail—perhaps of bodily pain, certainly of mental toil and preparation for His future service.

Such a public life as His could not have been lived without due training. Certainly it was one main point in His preparation that He was not without spiritual conflicts and struggles, which must have involved suffering to such a nature as His was. No sooner does He appear on the stage of action and the Spirit of God descends upon Him in the waters of baptism than He is hurried off to a forty days' fast in the wilderness and to a prolonged and terrible conflict with His great enemy and ours. Of that time we may truly say that "He suffered, being tempted."

We cannot tell how much our Lord suffered even in the brightest portion of His career, for always was He "despised and rejected of men; a man of sorrows, and acquainted with grief." We cannot go into all the details of His life, but I think you may see that, even in the very smoothest part of it, He suffered. And Peter does well thus to sum it up, "Christ suffered."

"Unparalleled Suffering," Metropolitan Tabernacle Pulpit, No. 2573 (1883)

106

THE ANTIDOTE
FOR ANXIETY

Now the God of hope fill you with all joy and peace in believing.
ROMANS 15:13

Oh, what a blessed thing it is to feel that you have scripture at your back! Many saints that I have read of have asked, when dying, to have their fingers laid upon some precious promise of the Word, and they have thus witnessed to their conviction that the passage was the very truth of God to their souls.

You know how you take one another's word and trust to it. And when you get a note of hand in black and white from a good tradesman, you do not mistrust it. Then shall we ever mistrust the black and white of God—the record of His dear Son which He has given us in holy scripture? No. Nor will we mistrust the peace that comes into our heart through believing it.

And then, my brethren, also mark that our peace is founded on God's testimony concerning His Son. He tells us, in this Book, that the Only Begotten took upon Him human form and came down among men—that, being here, He lived the life of a servant and at the last, taking upon Him man's sin and as the Substitute for guilty men, He went up to the cross and there bore His Father's wrath, dying in the place of the guilty, "the just for the unjust, that he might bring us to God."

I recollect how I grasped that truth when I first understood it—it was that doctrine of substitution which brought peace to my troubled spirit. I saw that if Christ died for me, then I should not die. And that if He paid my debt, it was paid and I was clear. And I knew that this was the case as soon as I believed in Him. So I did believe in Him and I was filled with "peace in believing."

Our faith is, indeed, well-founded and can be abundantly justified. Faith in Christ is nothing but common sense sanctified of God. It may be common sense to trust some banker who has long maintained his credit and not to be always worrying about whether he is solvent or not—but it is infinitely greater common sense to trust God, to trust His Son, to trust His Spirit, to trust His Word.

"Peace in Believing," Metropolitan Tabernacle Pulpit, No. 2626 (1882)

GROUNDLESS FEARS

Behold, I have graven thee upon the palms of my hands; thy walls are continually before me.
Isaiah 49:16

Dear friends, our complaints of God are generally groundless. We get into a state of mind in which we say, "God has forsaken us," when He is really dealing with us more than He was wont to do. A child who is feeling the strokes of the rod is very foolish to say, "My father has forgotten me." No, those very blows, under which he is smarting, are reminders that his father does not forget him—and your trials and your troubles, your depressions and your sorrows, are tokens that you are not forgotten of God.

Besides, dear friend, you have had some comforts though you have had many sorrows. You can say, "Comforts mingle with my sighs." Do not forget that. It is not all gall and wormwood; there is so much honey as greatly to mitigate the bitterness. Think of that, and do not obstinately stand to a word which, perhaps, you spoke in haste. If you have said, "My Lord hath forgotten me," call back the word, for it cannot be true. You have slandered Him who can never forget one of His own people. And if you have said, "Jehovah hath forsaken me," again I ask you to call back the evil and false word, and eat it. Never let it be heard again, for it is impossible that Jehovah should change or that the immutable love of His infinite heart should ever die out.

Does the vine say, "The vinedresser has forsaken me because he prunes me so sharply"? Does the invalid say, "The physician has forgotten me because he gives me such bitter medicine"? Shall the patient beneath the knife say, "The surgeon has forsaken me because he cuts even to the bone"? You see at once that there is no reasonableness about such talk, so dismiss it at once.

"Judge not the Lord" by outward providences any more than "by feeble sense," but trust Him even when you can see no trace of His goodness to you. "Let God be true, and" every circumstance, as well as "every man, a liar," for God must keep His promise to His people. He is immutable—He cannot possibly change. He must be true to every word that has gone forth out of His mouth.

"Neither Forsaken nor Forgotten," Metropolitan Tabernacle Pulpit, No. 2672 (1882)

A REASON TO REJOICE

Thou hast granted me life and favour.

JOB 10:12

The man who knows that his eternal future is secured by the unfailing grace of God may forever praise the Lord who has given him life. I find that in the Hebrew, this word *life* is in the plural— "Thou hast granted me lives"—and, blessed be God, we who believe in Jesus have not only this natural life, which we share in common with all men, but the Holy Spirit has begotten in the hearts of believers a new life infinitely higher than mere natural life, a life which makes us akin to Christ, joint heirs with Him of the eternal inheritance which He is keeping for us in heaven.

Let us praise God, then, for life, and especially for this higher life if it is ours. What a joy it is to live in this respect! You know that when a person is very sick and ill and can scarcely turn in bed or lift a hand, when every sense is deprived of enjoyment and every vein or nerve becomes a road for the hot feet of pain to travel over, then life is hardly to be called life. But when God graciously raises us up from sickness, we ought to bless Him for giving us life again— prolonged, restored, enjoyable life—and when the heart itself is sick, when the spirit flags, and the soul is ready to burst with inward grief, then the spiritual life seems scarcely to be life. But when, through the mercy of God, the Holy Spirit comes to us and applies the pardoning blood of Jesus to our heart and conscience, and whispers peace to our troubled spirit so that we can read our title clear to mansions in the skies, then our spiritual life is life indeed. We run, we leap, we fly, we would scarcely exchange for the bliss of angels the joy which the spiritual life brings to us at such times, and we bless and magnify the Lord who has granted us this higher life, this life so blessed, so superlatively blessed that, even here below, it makes us anticipate and realize some of the glory of heaven itself.

"A Song and a Solace," Metropolitan Tabernacle Pulpit, No. 2682 (1881)

COMFORTING PROVIDENCE

Thy visitation hath preserved my spirit.
JOB 10:12

You know, in this world, we see the wrong side of the carpet that is being woven. We are like Hannah More in the carpet factory, when she said to the workman, "I cannot see any design. There seem to be a great number of loose pieces of wool, but I cannot perceive any pattern or order." "No, madam," said the man, "of course you cannot—because you are standing on the wrong side of the carpet. If you will come to the other side, you will then see it all."

We are on the wrong side at present, but God will take us to the other side by and by. And then we shall each one say, "O my Lord, how wrongly did I judge Thee! I thought Thy visitation would have crushed me, but it preserved my spirit."

There are other visitations, however, such as the visitations of consolation. You and I must have known times when our spirits have gone down below zero, when no earthly friend could comfort us, and we could not think of any source of consolation for ourselves. Just then, some unnoticed promise of the Word of God has dropped into our soul with charming effect. It was, perhaps, but a sentence of half a dozen words, but they came from God the Holy Ghost, the comforter, and they were so powerfully applied to our spirit that we said, "I cannot tell what the divine will may be concerning me, or however dark and dreary may be the valley of the shadow of death through which I shall have to pass. But God's rod and staff are evidently with me, and they will comfort me in the most trying hour, and my Lord Himself will surely bring me through all my tribulations."

Cannot some of you say that your blessed Savior, who has suffered for you and who understands all your griefs, has come and bound up your broken hearts and given you unfailing comfort when you were in such sorrow that you feared you would have lost your reason and perhaps even taken your own life? But here you are, the living to praise Him, and to say, "Thy visitation by way of comfort has preserved my spirit."

"A SONG AND A SOLACE," METROPOLITAN TABERNACLE PULPIT, NO. 2682 (1881)

THE SUN STILL SHINES

These things hast thou hid in thine heart:
I know that this is with thee.
JOB 10:13

[God] spent the best He had upon us, and do you think that after that He will ever leave us? All the goodness of the past is an infallible guarantee that He will be good to us even to the end, according to that word concerning the Lord Jesus: "Having loved his own which were in the world, he loved them unto the end." That is one meaning of the verse.

But next, I think that the words, "And these things hast thou hid in thine heart: I know that this is with thee," have this meaning: that God sometimes hides His favor and love in His heart, yet they are there still. At times, it may be that you get no glimpse of His face or that you see no smile upon it. When that is my experience, I love to turn to that verse in the 63rd Psalm: "Because thou hast been my help, therefore in the shadow of thy wings will I rejoice."

It is all shadow, shadow, shadow—no sunshine. I cannot see my God, but the very shadow is the shadow of His wings, and as you may often see the chickens cower down beneath the mother hen and nestle there, so in the shadow of His wings will I rejoice. And you, dear friend, may share that blessed and safe shelter.

When there is no light, you shall walk on as steadily as

if seven suns were shining. When there is no comfortable assurance for you, when there is no temporal deliverance, when there is nothing for you out of the winepress or out of the barn, when there is no friend nor helper near you, when the fig tree does not blossom, when you have no flocks and your herds are cut off by the storm, when God's mercy seems to be clean gone forever, and His promises all appear to fail, it is not really so.

> *He hides the purpose of His grace*
> *To make it better known.*

The Lord is gracious, and full of compassion. Therefore, O tried child of God, learn what Job here teaches us—that these things are still hidden in the heart of God, and that eternal love holds fast to the objects of its choice.

"A Song and a Solace," Metropolitan Tabernacle Pulpit, No. 2682 (1881)

GROWING THROUGH THE PAIN

Knowing this, that the trying of your faith worketh
patience. But let patience have her perfect work,
that ye may be perfect and entire, wanting nothing.
JAMES 1:3–4

Railway men do not build bridges over rivers without an intention of sending engines and trains across them—and God does not give faith without an intention of letting it be tried. And He wants you to know, when He does try you or permit others to try you, that He still loves you. When He leaves you for a little while in the dark, He loves you just as much as when you were in the light.

A little child cries, and says that her mother does not love her because she has put her to bed and gone downstairs and left her in the dark. She will always be a baby if the mother stays there with a candle by the hour together till she gets to sleep. The mother wants her child to grow into a woman, and she trains her accordingly. So is it with us. God does often humor our littleness and weakness by doing many kind things to us as we do to poor feeble little children. But He wants us to grow up and become men and women in Christ Jesus, and to be strong in the Lord.

I pray that you, my dear brethren and sisters, may be stalwart Christians of this sort. You see, if our faith is to depend upon our disposition, our joy or our sorrow, it will be always fluctuating, up and down, and we shall be apt to think that we may be saved today and lost tomorrow. That is not the teaching of the Bible. When you are on the mountain with Christ, you are safe—but when you are at the bottom of the valley with Christ, you are just as safe. When you sit at the table with Christ, you are safe; and so you are if you should be at sea with Christ in the vessel. Only have faith in Him and say, "My God, Thy will towards me to give me life, and favor, and preservation, may be hidden, but it is still in Thine heart. 'I know that this is with thee.'"

"A Song and a Solace," Metropolitan Tabernacle Pulpit, No. 2682 (1881)

WORDLESS PRAYERS

When the poor and needy seek water, and there is none,
and their tongue faileth for thirst, I the LORD will hear
them, I the God of Israel will not forsake them.
ISAIAH 41:17

You feel, perhaps, as if you could not pray. Well then, now turn yourself to God; rest yourself on God. You feel that all is over with you, that your case is desperate; then roll yourself upon the living God. This is the point to which He means to bring you, so do not let even your desire to pray be an obstacle between the Lord and your soul.

If you cannot utter a word, pray in this sense: that your very heart, with unutterable groanings, pours itself out like water before the living God. This is where He would have us come, and oftentimes, it needs all this bursting of the tempest, all this sorrow, all this grief, before the Lord can get us to really speak with Him—not in words, but from our very soul.

The prayer which is hidden away in the text—for although there is no mention of prayer in it, yet it is hidden away there—is the prayer of inward thirst. You know that it is useless to say to a man who is in distress of soul, "You must groan every morning, and you must groan every night." No, no, he groans when he cannot help it, and though I wish that all would have their special seasons for prayer, yet I do believe that the most mighty prayer in the world is that which cannot be timed or regulated but which comes out because the suppliant must pray.

"Oh, God!" There may be more real prayer in that spontaneous outcry, when it is forced out of you by the overwhelming sense of your need, than there is when you put yourself into a comfortable position and kneel down to pray. For sometimes you may get up from that posture and say to yourself, "There, I think I prayed very well," yet all the while, there may not have been any true prayer in it. But when, at another time, you say, "O Lord, I cannot pray, I feel as if I could not pray"—why, dear man, you are praying! You are praying with all your might.

———————

"WORDLESS PRAYERS HEARD IN HEAVEN,"
METROPOLITAN TABERNACLE PULPIT, NO. 2696 (1881)

PRAYER: THE PATHWAY TO PEACE

And there appeared an angel unto him
from heaven, strengthening him.

LUKE 22:43

Scarcely had our Savior prayed before the answer to His petition came. It reminds us of Daniel's supplication, and of the angelic messenger who was caused to fly so swiftly that as soon as the prayer had left the prophet's lips, Gabriel stood there with the reply to it. So, brethren and sisters, whenever your times of trial come, always betake yourselves to your knees.

Whatever shape your trouble may take—if, to you, it should even seem to be a faint representation of your Lord's agony in Gethsemane—put yourselves into the same posture as that in which He sustained the great shock that came upon Him. Kneel down and cry to your Father who is in heaven, who is able to save you from death, who will prevent the trial from utterly destroying you, who will give you strength that you may be able to endure it, and will bring you through it to the praise of the glory of His grace.

Possibly, you have sometimes said, "I feel so sorrowful that I cannot pray." Nay, brother, that is the very time when you must pray. As the spices, when bruised, give forth all the more fragrance because of the bruising, so let the sorrow of your spirit cause it to send forth the more fervent prayer to the God who is both able and willing to deliver you.

You must express your sorrow in one way or another, so let it not be expressed in murmuring but in supplication. It is a vile temptation, on the part of Satan, to keep you away from the mercy seat when you have most need to go there, but do not yield to that temptation. Pray till you can pray, and if you find that you are not filled with the Spirit of supplication, use whatever measure of the sacred bedewing you have—and so, by and by, you shall have the baptism of the Spirit and prayer shall become to you a happier and more joyful exercise than it is at present. Our Savior said to His disciples, "My soul is exceeding sorrowful, even unto death," yet then, above all times, He was in an agony of prayer—and in proportion to the intensity of His sorrow was the intensity of His supplication.

"THE WEAKENED CHRIST STRENGTHENED,"
METROPOLITAN TABERNACLE PULPIT, NO. 2769 (1881)

IN YOUR DARKEST HOUR

Surely he shall deliver thee from the snare of the fowler,
and from the noisome pestilence. He shall cover thee
with his feathers, and under his wings shalt thou trust:
his truth shall be thy shield and buckler. Thou shalt not be
afraid for the terror by night; nor for the arrow that flieth
by day; nor for the pestilence that walketh in darkness;
nor for the destruction that wasteth at noonday.

PSALM 91:3–6

While you should be thankful for the least comforter, yet in your times of deepest need you may expect the greatest comforters to come to you. Let me remind you that an angel appeared to Joseph when Herod was seeking Christ's life. Then later, angels appeared to Christ when the devil had been tempting Him. And now, at Gethsemane, when there was a peculiar manifestation of diabolical malice, for it was the hour of the powers of darkness—then when the devil was loose and doing his utmost against Christ, an angel came from heaven to strengthen Him.

So when you are in your heaviest trials, you shall have your greatest strength. Perhaps you will have little to do with angels till you get into deep trouble, and then shall the promise be fulfilled: "He shall give his angels charge over thee, to keep thee in all thy ways. They shall bear thee up in their hands, lest thou dash thy foot against a stone." They are always ready to be your keepers, but in the matter of spiritual strengthening, these holy spirits may have little to do with some of you until you stand foot to foot with Apollyon and have to fight stern battles with the evil one himself.

It is worthwhile to go through rough places to have angels to bear you up. It is worthwhile to go to Gethsemane, if there we may have angels from heaven to strengthen us. So be of good comfort, brethren, whatever lies before you. The darker your experience is, the brighter will be that which comes out of it.

The disciples feared as they entered the cloud on the Mount of Transfiguration, but when they had passed right into it, they saw Jesus, Moses, and Elijah in glory. O you, who are the true followers of Christ, fear not the clouds that lower darkly over you, for you shall see the brightness behind them and the Christ in them—and blessed shall your spirits be.

"THE WEAKENED CHRIST STRENGTHENED,"
METROPOLITAN TABERNACLE PULPIT, No. 2769 (1881)

WHEN SORROW STRIKES

O my God, my soul is cast down within me:
therefore will I remember thee from the land of
Jordan, and of the Hermonites, from the hill Mizar.
PSALM 42:6

Even the apostle Paul was not exempt from doubts and fears, for he wrote, "We were troubled on every side; without were fightings, within were fears"; and on another occasion, "I keep under my body, and bring it into subjection: lest that by any means, when I have preached to others, I myself should be a castaway." The man after God's own heart, even David—a man of experience so deep that none of us can fully decipher, much less rival, it—a man of love so fervent that few of us can do more than aspire to catch the hallowed flame—nevertheless, had to cry aloud, and that very often, "O my God, my soul is cast down within me!"

"But," says one, "this deathlike faintness comes upon me so often, therefore I cannot be a child of God." Ay, but let me tell you that possibly it will come more often yet—or should it come more seldom, if you shall have weeks of pleasure or even months of enjoyment—it is possible that your doubts will then be doubled in intensity, and your soul will yet have greater trials to experience. So great a Savior is provided for our deliverance that we must expect to have great castings down from which we need to be delivered.

Why, believer, what are one half of the promises worth if we are not the subjects of doubts and fears? Why has Jehovah given us so many *shalls* and *wills* but because He knew that we should have so many accursed *ifs* and *peradventures*? He would never have given us such a well-filled storehouse of comfort if He had not foreseen that we should have a full measure of sorrow. God never makes greater provision than will be needed, so as there is an abundance of consolations, we may rest assured that there will be an abundance of tribulations also. There will be much fear and casting down to each of us before we see the face of God in heaven. This disease of soul dejection is common to all the saints. There are none of God's people who altogether escape it.

"SWEET STIMULANTS FOR THE FAINTING SOUL," METROPOLITAN TABERNACLE PULPIT, NO. 2798 (1860)

WHEN FAITH AND GRIEF COEXIST

For our light affliction, which is but for
a moment, worketh for us a far more
exceeding and eternal weight of glory.
2 CORINTHIANS 4:17

The highest joy and the deepest sorrow may be found in the Christian; and the truest faith and yet the most grievous doubts may meet together in the child of God. Of course, they only meet there to make his heart a battlefield—but there they may meet, and his faith may be real while his doubts are grievous.

I would remark, yet further, that not only is it possible for a man to thus be cast down and yet to have true faith all the while, but he may actually be growing in grace while he is cast down—ay, and he may really be standing higher when he is cast down than he did when he stood upright. Strange riddle! But we who have passed through this experience know that it is true. When we are flat on our faces, we are generally the nearest to heaven. When we sink the lowest in our own esteem, we rise the highest in fellowship with Christ and in knowledge of Him. Someone said, "The way to heaven is not upward, but downward." There is some truth in the saying; though it is upward in Christ, it is downward in self, as Dr. Watts sings:

> *The more Thy glories strike mine eyes,*
> *The humbler I shall lie.*

The inverse is equally true: the humbler I lie at my Savior's feet, the more His glories strike my eyes. This very casting down into the dust sometimes enables the Christian to bear a blessing from God which he could not have carried if he had been standing upright. There is such a thing as being crushed with a load of grace, bowed down with a tremendous weight of benedictions, having such blessings from God that if our soul were not cast down by them, they would be the ruin of us.

The Christian life is a riddle, and most surely are God's people familiar with that riddle in their experience. They must work it out before they can understand it. So I say again that this casting down is consistent with the most elevated degree of piety.

"SWEET STIMULANTS FOR THE FAINTING SOUL,"
METROPOLITAN TABERNACLE PULPIT, NO. 2798 (1860)

GIVING THE BATTLE TO GOD

The LORD shall fight for you, and ye shall hold your peace.
EXODUS 14:14

The first remedy for soul dejection is a reference of ourselves to God—as David says, "O my God, my soul is cast down within me: therefore will I remember thee." If you have a trouble to bear, the best thing for you to do is not to try to bear it at all, but to cast it upon the shoulders of the Eternal. If you have anything that perplexes you, the simplest plan for you will be not to try to solve the difficulty, but to seek direction from heaven concerning it.

Remember how men act when they are concerned in a lawsuit—if they are wise, they do not undertake the case themselves. They know our familiar proverb, "He who is his own lawyer has a fool for his client," so they take their case to someone who is able to deal with it, and leave it with him.

Well, now, if men have not sufficient skill to deal with matters that come before our courts of law, do you think that you have skill enough to plead in the court of heaven against such a cunning old attorney as the devil, who has earned the name of "the accuser of the brethren" (and well deserves the title)? Never try to plead against him, but put your case into the hands of our great Advocate. For "if any man sin, we have an Advocate with the Father, Jesus Christ the righteous."

Often, when I call to see a troubled Christian, do you know what he is almost sure to say? "Oh, sir, I do not feel this—and I do fear that—and I cannot help thinking the other!" That great *I* is the root of all our sorrows: what I feel or what I do not feel, that is enough to make anyone miserable. It is a wise plan to say to such a one, "Oh, yes! I know that all you say about yourself is only too true, but now, let me hear what you have to say about Christ. For the next twenty-four hours at least, leave off thinking about yourself, and think only of Christ."

"Sweet Stimulants for the Fainting Soul,"
Metropolitan Tabernacle Pulpit, No. 2798 (1860)

ANXIOUS HEARTS RECEIVE GOD'S POWER

He giveth power to the faint.
Isaiah 40:29

See how tenderly the Lord deals with His fainting people. He does not desert them when they are faint, saying, "They are no longer any use to Me. They can do nothing for Me, I will leave them where they are." No, but "He giveth power to the faint." Observe that He does not merely comfort the faint, or rebuke or reprove them. That would not help them much when they were fainting. But He does what we cannot do for fainting people: He gives them power. That is the best way to deliver them from their faintness. Even if no cheering word is whispered in your ear, if power is given to you, if your pulse is quickened and your spirit is filled with new energy, your faintness will soon be over. This is what the Lord does for you when "he giveth power to the faint."

What sort of power does He give to the faint? Well, you may be sure that He does not give them any of their own. That has all gone from them. The very image of death is stamped upon them. See how pale they look; note how the blood seems to have fled from their faces; their own power has all gone from them. So, my brothers and sisters, when the Lord gives power to the faint, it is His own power that

He gives to them. What a blessing it is to feel that it is His power that is working in you!

When God gives power to the faint, you may rest assured that it will be sufficient for the emergency, for He has all-sufficient power—and He never gives to His people merely half the power or a tenth of the power that they need, but He gives them all the power that they require. His promise is "As thy days, so shall thy strength be."

The mercy is that the power that God gives is a power that the devil can neither defeat nor take away. If He has given you that power, it shall be yours as long as you need it. That power neither man nor devil can take away from you. But through it, you shall be enabled to tread down all your adversaries and conquer all your difficulties.

"Causes and Cure of Fainting," Metropolitan Tabernacle Pulpit, No. 2812 (1877)

YOUR TRIAL IS NOT IN VAIN

*Who comforteth us in all our tribulation, that we may
be able to comfort them which are in any trouble, by the
comfort wherewith we ourselves are comforted of God.*
2 CORINTHIANS 1:4

There is wondrous power in the weakness which leads us to
faint away on the bosom of God, and so to be made strong
in the Lord and in the power of His might—just to swoon
into unconsciousness and then to find our all-sufficiency in
our God—to get out of life of a carnal kind by swooning
into the image of death and then being raised into newness
of life by the resurrection power of the Lord Jesus Christ.
That is the kind of power which God gives to the faint.

Why is it that He gives this power to the faint? Well,
I think it is because in His great goodness, He looks out
for those who need it most. As we, if we are wise, give our
alms to the most destitute, God gives His power to those
who require it most, those who are fainting for lack of it.
Then, next, He gives it to them because they will praise
Him most for it. When the fainting ones receive the power
that God gives to them, they will say that it is of the Lord,
and not of themselves. They will be the people to receive
this power because they will be sure to use it. I think that
when a person who has been faint receives power from God,
he will likely be sympathetic, tender, and gentle towards
others—at least, that is how he should be.

I have known a dear brother who has never had an hour's illness in his life seek to sympathize with me when I have been in great pain, but it was like an elephant trying to pick up a pin—he cannot do it; it is not in his line. But he who has been faint, and then has received power from God, is the man who knows what faintness means—and so is gentle towards other fainting ones as a nurse is with the little child committed to her charge. Hence, the Lord entrusts power to His fainting children because He knows that they will be sympathetic and use it wisely and well.

"CAUSES AND CURE OF FAINTING," METROPOLITAN TABERNACLE PULPIT, NO. 2812 (1877)

OUR HIDING PLACE

And a man shall be as an hiding place from
the wind, and a covert from the tempest.
Isaiah 32:2

I invite all of you who are afraid of the storms of doubt or
trial or temptation or of the wrath of God to put your trust
in the Lord Jesus Christ—because, being God, He is omnipotent and therefore nothing can be too difficult for Him.

Yet, as the text says, "a man shall be as an hiding place
from the wind, and a covert from the tempest," I remark
that Christ is truly a man. Oh, how often, in the thought of
Christ's real humanity, has my soul found a hiding place from
all manner of storms! "God"—the word is great! "God"—
the idea is sublime! The great eternal Jehovah, who made
the heavens and the earth and who bears them up by His
unaided power, who rides upon the stormy sky and puts a
bit into the mouth of the raging tempest—how shall I, a
poor worm of the dust, draw nigh to such a God as this?

The answer quickly comes: "He has been pleased to reveal
himself in the Man Christ Jesus." "God was in Christ, recon-
ciling the world unto himself, not imputing their trespasses
unto them." Why should I dread to appear before God, now
that in the person of His Son, Jesus Christ, there is a link
between my manhood and His deity?

The awful gulf that sin had made is bridged, and now

I perceive how near God comes down to man and how closely He lifts up man to Himself. Jesus Christ was truly man. With the exception of being free from sin, He was in no respect different from ourselves—and at this moment, though He occupies the very throne of God in glory, His sympathies run towards us.

> *He knows what sore temptations mean,*
> *For He has felt the same.*

He is ready to succor us, for His delights are still with the sons of men. He became a man because He loved men. God has such affection for our race that He has married our nature to Himself. Oh, what joy there ought to be in our hearts because of this! The very fact that God has become incarnate makes Him to be a hiding place from the wind, and a covert from the tempest.

"OUR HIDING PLACE," METROPOLITAN
TABERNACLE PULPIT, NO. 2856 (1877)

DEATH IS NOTHING TO FEAR

O death, where is thy sting? O grave, where is thy victory?
1 Corinthians 15:55

The wind howls sadly out yonder among the tombs in the cemetery. One would scarcely choose to spend a night there alone among the dead, but even that mournful wind, when it is heard by the ear of faith, has music in it. That ancient message is yet to be fulfilled: "Thy dead men shall live, together with my dead body shall they arise." This is what Christ says to us, so we need not stand by the pious dead and weep as those without hope, but we may already begin to anticipate the dawning of that glorious morning when, at the summons of the descending Savior, "the dead in Christ shall rise first: then we which are alive and remain shall be caught up together with them in the clouds, to meet the Lord in the air; and so shall we always be with the Lord."

Jesus, therefore, as our Representative, is a hiding place to us from all the winds which would come to us by the way of the sepulchre. We are not afraid to die, for Jesus lives—and He said to His disciples, "Because I live, ye shall live also." He has also gone up into heaven, in His glorified body; He ascended up on high, there to appear in the presence of God for us.

So whenever you have any dread about the future, recollect that you will be where He is. If you are a believer in

Him, you must ascend to heaven even as He has done; and as He sits upon His throne, even so shall you; and as He is perfected in glory, even so must you be.

If you hide behind this rampart of stupendous rock—this mighty mound of divine consolation—it matters not what winds may rage or what storms may roar; you may rest in security and serenity behind the great representative man who is "as an hiding place from the wind, and a covert from the tempest." Our earthly friends may die, but we shall never lose our best friend. All merely human comforters will fail us sooner or later, but He will always abide true and steadfast to all who rely upon Him.

"Our Hiding Place," Metropolitan Tabernacle Pulpit, No. 2856 (1877)

THE "WHAT IF" CURE

Take therefore no thought for the morrow: for the morrow shall take thought for the things of itself. Sufficient unto the day is the evil thereof.
MATTHEW 6:34

The great drama of this world's history draws towards its close. We know not when it will end, for it is not for us "to know the times or the seasons, which the Father hath put in his own power"; but there comes to us, as a clear, ringing message out of the deep mystery of the future, the voice of our Savior, saying, "Surely I come quickly," to which our glad response is "Even so, come, Lord Jesus!"

I cannot foretell to what a state of anarchy or of despotism this world may yet come. I cannot forecast the ultimate issues of great wars and conflicts between divers nations, but the saints of God shall always have a hiding place from every stormy wind that shall ever blow. "The Lord himself shall descend from heaven with a shout, with the voice of the archangel, and with the trump of God." "He cometh to judge the earth: he shall judge the world with righteousness, and the people with his truth."

There shall come a day when that ancient prophecy shall be fulfilled: "He shall live, and to him shall be given of the gold of Sheba: prayer also shall be made for him continually, and daily shall he be praised." There shall yet come a halcyon period when they shall hang the useless helmet high and study war no more, but the silver trumpet of the blessed jubilee shall sound aloud, for Christ—the great Prince of Peace—shall then have returned to reign and His unsuffering kingdom shall know no end. This is the world's hope, that the people's Christ, the man chosen out of the people, the lover of mankind, the great philanthropist, the divine man, shall come and reign among His loyal subjects and be to them "as an hiding place from the wind, and a covert from the tempest."

To sum all up, beloved, I do not know what your storms—inwardly or outwardly—may be, or what may be your special dread or terror. But if you hide away in the Man Christ Jesus, you will find that He will afford you shelter from every trouble that can possibly befall you.

"Our Hiding Place," Metropolitan Tabernacle Pulpit, No. 2856 (1877)

OUR STABLE HOPE IN UNSTABLE TIMES

Because thy lovingkindness is better than life, my lips shall praise thee.
PSALM 63:3

Whenever there is a cross to be carried by any of Christ's followers, He always bears the heavy end on His own shoulders. He always takes the bleak side of the hill Himself, and His disciples may be well content to follow when they have so good a Master to lead the way.

When John the Baptist was put to death, his disciples took up his body and went and told Jesus. That was the best thing they could have done. When the little baby dies, dear mother, take up its body and go and tell Jesus. When you are out of employment, working man, and the supply of bread is short in the home, go and tell Jesus. He will sympathize with you, for He also was anhungred. And when others of the trials of life come upon any of you, do not hesitate as to what you will do—but if you have hidden behind Him on account of sin, go and hide in Him on account of sorrow, for this Man shall always be a hiding place from every stormy wind that blows if you do but know how to go and trust in Him.

Come to my Lord Jesus Christ, my dear fellow men, because He is an effectual hiding place. Many of us have tried Him and proved that He is all that I have said. There have been millions upon millions of His saints, in all ages, who have cast upon Him their entire life-burden, and He has never failed to relieve any one of them yet. I have stood by the bedside of many dying Christians, but to this moment I have never heard one of them say that Christ had played him false.

There are hosts of biographies of Christians published— did you ever find in any of them a single instance in which a believer in Christ found himself deserted and forsaken by his Savior? No, but on the contrary, the testimonies are heaped up far beyond any evidence that ever could be demanded in a court of law—and they prove, beyond all question, that Christ helps His children in all their emergencies and delivers them in every time of trouble.

"OUR HIDING PLACE," METROPOLITAN
TABERNACLE PULPIT, NO. 2856 (1877)

FINANCIAL CONCERNS

Neither be ye of doubtful mind.
LUKE 12:29

Our Savior's injunction means, "Do not be anxious about your temporal affairs." Be prudent—you have no right to spend the money of other people, nor yet your own, in wastefulness. You are to be careful and discreet, for every Christian should remember that he is only a steward and that he is accountable to his Master for whatever he has and the use he makes of it. But when you have done your best with your little, do not worry because you cannot make it more.

You cannot make a shilling into a sovereign, but be thankful if you have the shilling—and if you sometimes find that you must live from hand to mouth, remember that you are not the first child of God who has had his manna every morning, nor the first of God's servants to have bread and flesh in the morning and bread and flesh in the evening with nothing to lay by for the morrow. If this is your case, be not staggered and astonished, as though some new thing had happened to you, and do not begin to fret and fume and worry and trouble yourself about what you cannot help. Can you alter it with all your worrying?

Have you—you who are in the habit of worrying and fretting—ever made any profit by doing so? How much a year do you think that anybody would give you for all your fretting? How much has it brought you in? Come, brother, if it is a good business, I would like to go into partnership with you—but I should like first to know something about your profits. As I look at your face, I notice that it is care-worn and anxious. That does not seem to indicate that the business is a profitable one. If I listen to your speech, I hear you murmuring a great deal instead of praising God. That does not seem to me to be a profitable concern.

In fact, as far as I have ascertained, either by my own experience or by the observation of others, I have never discovered that anxiety has comforted anybody or that it has brought any grist to the mill or any meal to the barrel. Well, if a thing does not pay, what is the good of it?

"ANXIETY, AMBITION, INDECISION," METROPOLITAN
TABERNACLE PULPIT, NO. 2871 (1876)

GOD'S WORRY-ERASING FORGIVENESS

There is forgiveness with thee.
PSALM 130:4

Here is a most cheering announcement, "There is forgiveness with thee."

This announcement has great force and value, because it is most certainly true. When a man hears some news which pleases him, he loses that pleasure if he has reason to suspect that it is not true. The first questions you ask, when someone tells you of some good fortune that concerns you, are of this sort: "Are you quite sure it is so? Can you give me good authority for your assertion?"

Well, this news is certainly true for it is consistent with God's very nature. He is a gracious God. "He delighteth in mercy." Mercy was the last of His attributes that He was able to reveal. He could be great and good when the world was made, but He could not be merciful until sin had marred His perfect handiwork. There must be an offense committed before there can be mercy displayed towards the offender. Mercy, then, I may say, is God's Benjamin—His last born, His favored one, the son of His right hand.

I never read that He delighteth in power or that He delighteth in justice, but I do read, "He delighteth in mercy." It is the attribute that is sweetest to Himself to exercise.

When He goes forth to punish, as He must, His feet are, as it were, shod with iron—but when He comes to manifest His mercy, He rideth, as David says, "upon the wings of the wind." He delighteth to be gracious; therefore, I feel sure that there is forgiveness with Him.

If any of you doubt whether there is forgiveness with God, I pray you to stand on Calvary (in imagination) and to look into the wounds of Jesus—gaze upon His nail-pierced hands and feet, His thorn-crowned brow, and look right into His heart, where the soldier's spear was thrust and blood and water flowed out for the double cleansing of all who trust Him. O Christ of God, it could not be that You should die and yet that sinners cannot be forgiven! It would be a monstrous thing that You should have bled to death and yet that no sinner should be saved by that death. It cannot be—there must be forgiveness, there is forgiveness, since Jesus died, "the just for the unjust, that he might bring us to God."

"FORGIVENESS AND FEAR," METROPOLITAN
TABERNACLE PULPIT, NO. 2882 (1876)

146

CHEER UP—
GOD LOVES YOU!

These things have I spoken unto you, that my joy might remain in you, and that your joy might be full.
JOHN 15:11

The joy of Jesus is, first, the joy of abiding in His Father's love. He knows that His Father loves Him—that He never did anything else but love Him—that He loved Him or ever the earth was—that He loved Him when He was in the manger and that He loved Him when He was on the cross. Now that is the joy which Christ gives to you—the joy of knowing that your Father loves you.

Let me stop a little while, that you, who are really believers in the Lord Jesus Christ, may just roll that sweet morsel under your tongue—the everlasting God loves you! I have known the time when I have felt as if I could leap up at the very thought of God's love to me. That He pities you and cares for you, you can understand. But that He loves you—well, if that does not make your joy full, there is nothing that can.

Christ's joy was also the joy of hallowed friendship. He said to His disciples, "Henceforth I call you not servants; for the servant knoweth not what his Lord doeth: but I have called you friends; for all things that I have heard of my Father I have made known unto you." The friends of Jesus are those who are taken by Him into most intimate fellowship—to lean upon His breast and to become His constant companions.

Our Lord Jesus Christ has great joy in being on the most friendly terms with His people, and have not you also great joy in being on such friendly terms with Him? You are going to sit and feast with Him presently at His own table. He calls you no more His servant, but His friend. Does not that fact make you rejoice with exceeding joy? What is your heart made of if it does not leap with joy at such an assurance as that? You are beloved of the Lord and a friend of the Son of God! Kings might well be willing to give up their crowns if they could have such bliss as this.

"CHRIST'S JOY AND OURS," METROPOLITAN
TABERNACLE PULPIT, No. 2935 (1875)

GOD'S RELIEVING PARDON

Son, be of good cheer; thy sins be forgiven thee.
MATTHEW 9:2

If your sin is pardoned, it is true concerning you that no good thing will God withhold from you who walk uprightly; and that all things work together for good to you who love God, to you who are the called according to His purpose. Everything between here and heaven is secured by the covenant of grace for your best benefit, and you can sing:

> *If sin be pardon'd, I'm secure;*
> *Death hath no sting beside:*
> *The law gives sin its damning power;*
> *But Christ, my ransom, died.*

You shall never have a need but God will assuredly supply it since He has already bestowed on you the major blessing, the all-comprehending blessing of forgiveness. Covenant mercies follow each other like the links of a chain: "Who forgiveth all thine iniquities; who healeth all thy diseases; who redeemeth thy life from destruction; who crowneth thee with lovingkindness and tender mercies; who satisfieth thy mouth with good things; so that thy youth is renewed like the eagle's." Do you think that God forgives men their sins and then leaves them to perish? Such cruel "mercy" would be more worthy of a demon than of the Deity. Pardon is the pledge of everlasting love, and the pledge will never be forfeited.

"Alas!" cries one, "perhaps, after the Lord has forgiven me, He may yet turn again, and punish me." Listen: "The gifts and calling of God are without repentance." That is, God never repents of what He does in the way of grace. If He forgives, He forgives once for all and forever. It would be blasphemy to represent God as making a transient truce with men instead of an eternal peace.

The Lord casts the iniquities of His people into the depths of the sea, and their transgressions He remembers against them no more forever. Is not this a blessed act of grace? It secures the removal of all the evil results of sin and is the guarantee of all that will be needed this side of heaven—yea, and of glory forever. If you do but hear Jesus say, "Thy sins be forgiven thee," you may also hear Him say, "Be of good cheer," for there is everything in the fact of pardon to make your heart dance for joy.

"GOOD CHEER FROM FORGIVEN SIN," METROPOLITAN
TABERNACLE PULPIT, NO. 3016 (UNDATED)

LONELY, BUT NEVER ALONE

*Jesus answered them, Do ye now believe? Behold, the
hour cometh, yea, is now come, that ye shall be scattered,
every man to his own, and shall leave me alone: and
yet I am not alone, because the Father is with me.*
JOHN 16:31–32

No believer traverses all the road to heaven in company.
Lonely spots there must be here and there, though the
greater part of our heavenward pilgrimage is made cheerful
by the society of fellow travelers. Yet somewhere or other on
the road, every man will find narrow defiles and close places
where pilgrims must march in single file.

Sometimes the child of God endures loneliness arising
from the absence of godly society. It may be that in his early
days as a Christian, he mixed much with gracious persons,
was able to attend many of their meetings and to converse
in private with the excellent of the earth. But now his lot is
cast where he is as a sparrow alone on the housetop.

This is a very great trial to the Christian, an ordeal of the
most severe character. Even the strong may dread it and the
weak are sorely shaken by it. To such lonely ones, our Lord's
words, now before us, are commended with the prayer that
they may make them their own—"I am alone: and yet I am
not alone, because the Father is with me."

When Jacob was alone at Bethel, he laid down to sleep

and soon was in a region peopled by innumerable spirits, above whom was God Himself. That vision made the night at Bethel the least lonely season that Jacob ever spent. Your meditations, O solitary ones, as you read the Bible in secret, and your prayers, as you draw near to God in your lonely room and your Savior Himself in His blessed person, will be to you what the ladder was to Jacob.

The words of God's Book, made living to you, shall be to your mind the angels, and God Himself shall have fellowship with you. If you lament your loneliness, cure it by seeking heavenly company. If you have no companions below who are holy, seek all the more to commune with those who are in heaven, where Christ sits at the right hand of God.

"Christ's Loneliness and Ours," Metropolitan Tabernacle Pulpit, No. 3052 (Undated)

HOPE FOR THE BROKENHEARTED

He hath sent me to bind up the brokenhearted.
ISAIAH 61:1

My brokenhearted friend, suppose that all men forsake or forget you—God does not. His eye sees you, His heart feels for you, and His hand is able to deliver you. You are not friendless, nor will you be till the God of all consolation dies—and that can never be.

Christ's declaration should cheer the brokenhearted, again, because they often conclude that their case is beyond all help. "Ah!" says one, "even if I had a friend, he could not help me, for my case is beyond all succor. If I had fifty friends, they would not know how to minister to such mental disease as mine. I am too far gone for relief."

But hearken, my brokenhearted friend. You dare not say that anything is too hard for the Lord—though your despair would make you go a long way, yet it would not make you go so far as to say that God cannot help you. He it is that turns the night into morning, that stills the roaring of the sea, that puts a bit into the mouth of the tempest—then what can He not do? You cannot be in so forlorn a condition that God cannot help you.

This ought still further to comfort the poor desponding one because he often concludes that certainly God is against him. It is not so—if it were, then might the great bell toll out your knell, but my text says that the Lord has sent His Son, Jesus Christ, to bind up the brokenhearted. He is no enemy to you, or He would not have sent His Son to heal you.

So say we to you, poor brokenhearted one! If the Lord meant to destroy you, why did He send His Son to heal the brokenhearted, and to what end is the gospel sent, and why are you here to be tenderly wooed and assured that the Lord has deep designs of love toward just such troubled souls as you are? I believe that you will yet dance for joy of heart, that you will yet take down your harp from the willows, and like Miriam with her timbrel, that you will yet rejoice over the Egyptians whom you have feared but whom you shall see no more forever.

<hr>

"Binding Up Broken Hearts," Metropolitan Tabernacle Pulpit, No. 3104 (1874)

THE EXPERT HEART-HEALER

That it might be fulfilled which was spoken
by Esaias the prophet, saying, Himself took
our infirmities, and bare our sicknesses.
MATTHEW 8:17

Let me also tell you, O you brokenhearted ones, that God has sent one to heal your hearts who has already healed multitudes of others. People like a man of experience for the healing of the body, and experience is just as valuable for the healing of the soul. Jesus Christ has bound up millions of broken hearts, so He knows how to heal yours. He knows precisely where the malady is and what remedy to apply.

The Lord has also sent one who will not be discouraged or get irritated in His work of comforting you. Sometimes when we try to comfort a mourner, and he will not be comforted, we get impatient and do more hurt than good. There is many a man who has gone with the best intentions to try and cheer a diseased mind who has inflicted fresh wounds through his own impatience with the patient—but Jesus Christ "can have compassion on the ignorant, and on them that are out of the way."

He bears and forbears and is as gentle as a nurse with the children under her charge—and far more so. He will drive your sin out of you, and then He will take your sorrow away from you, or else give you the grace to enable you to bear it.

There never was anyone else who was like Jesus as the healer of the brokenhearted. If you could see Him here, in bodily presence, you would say, "That is the one to whom I can tell all my troubles." You know how it is recorded of Him that He "healed all that were sick; that it might be fulfilled which was spoken by Esaias the prophet, saying, Himself took our infirmities, and bore our sicknesses."

You may always come to Jesus; He will always be willing to hear your sad story, always be able to solve your difficulties, and always be able to relieve your distresses. This ought to comfort you, but I cannot make it do so. I am not sent to bind up the brokenhearted in the same sense in which Christ was. I am sent to be an instrument in His hand—but He must do the work, for He only can do it.

"Binding Up Broken Hearts," Metropolitan
Tabernacle Pulpit, No. 3104 (1874)

OUR GREATEST FEAR, ERASED

And deliver them who through fear of death
were all their lifetime subject to bondage.
Hebrews 2:15

Death to the believer is no penalty—it is a development from this time state to another and a higher one—a breaking of the shell that now confines us—a snapping of the cable that holds the vessel to the shore—a severing of the chain that holds the eagle down to the rock. Death releases us so that we may soar away to that land of light and love where Jesus is, as John Newton sings:

> *In vain my fancy strives to paint*
> *The moment after death,*
> *The glories that surround the saint*
> *When yielding up his breath.*

> *One gentle sigh the fetter breaks:*
> *We scarce can say, "They're gone!"*
> *Before the willing spirit takes*
> *Her mansion near the throne.*

Death to the believer is not an execution—it is his deliverance, his freedom from manumission and admission into the glory of God. Christ has taken away the fear of death from those who truly know Him by assuring us that our soul shall not die or become extinct. Because our souls shall never die, we are not afraid to venture into the world of spirits.

Then there is that master doctrine of the Christian faith which was not revealed to men in all its fullness until Jesus came. I mean the doctrine of the resurrection of the body. It is for this body that we have any fear—corruption, earth, and worms are its heritage—and it seems a hard thing that these eyes, which have seen the light, should be blinded in the mold; that these limbs, which have trodden the pilgrim path, should be able to move no longer.

But courage, believer! Your body shall rise again. Laid in the earth it may be, but kept in the earth it cannot be. The voice of nature bids you die, but the voice of the Omnipotent bids you live again. This is our consolation, that, as Jesus Christ died and rose again from the dead, "even so them also which sleep in Jesus will God bring with him."

"FEAR OF DEATH," METROPOLITAN
TABERNACLE PULPIT, NO. 3125 (1874)

DON'T ASSUME THE WORST

Thou knowest not what a day may bring forth.
PROVERBS 27:1

My friend, you are afraid tonight—you cannot enjoy anything you have because of this terrible and fearful shadow which has come across your path of an evil which you say is coming tomorrow, or in one or two months' time, or even in six months. Now, at least, you are not quite certain that it will come, for you know not what may be on the morrow. You are as alarmed and as afraid as if you were quite certain that it would appear.

But it is not so: "Thou knowest not what a day may bring forth," and since it is uncertain whether it shall be or not, had you not better leave your sorrow till it is certain? And meanwhile, leave the uncertain matter in the hand of God, whose divine purposes will be wise and good in the end, and will be even seen to be so! At the very least, slender as the comfort may be, yet there is still comfort in the fact that you know not what may be on the morrow.

Let us expand this thought a little to those of you who are fearing about tomorrow. We very often fear what never will occur. I think that the major part of our troubles are not those which God sends us, but those which we invent for ourselves. As the poet speaks of some who "Feel a thousand deaths in fearing one," so there are many who feel a thousand troubles in fearing one trouble—which trouble, perhaps, never will have any existence except in the workshop of their own misty brain. It is an ill task for a child to whip himself; it might be good for him to feel the whip from his father's hand, but it is of little service when the child applies it himself.

And yet, very often, the strokes which we dread never come from God's hand at all but are the pure inventions of our own imagination and our own unbelief working together. There are more who have to howl under the lash of unbelief than there are who have to weep under the gentle rod of God's providential dispensation.

"CHEER FOR DESPONDENCY," METROPOLITAN
TABERNACLE PULPIT, No. 3183 (UNDATED)

DEEP WATER,
DEEPER TRUST

When thou passest through the waters, I will be with thee.
Isaiah 43:2

These trials of yours shall be the winepress out of which shall come the wine of consolation to you. This furnace shall rob you of nothing but your dross, which you will be glad to be rid of—but your pure gold shall not be diminished by so much as a drachma, but shall only be the purer after it all.

And there is one thing more, supposing the trial does come: thy God has promised that, as thy days, so shall thy strength be. Has He not said it many times in His Word, "I will never leave thee, nor forsake thee"? He never did promise you freedom from trouble. He speaks of rivers, and of your going through them; He speaks of fires, and of your passing through them; but He has added, "When thou passest through the waters, I will be with thee; and through the rivers, they shall not overflow thee; when thou walkest through the fire, thou shalt not be burned; neither shall the flame kindle upon thee." What matters it to you, then, whether there be fire or not if you be not burned?

What matters it to you whether there are floods or not if you are not drowned? As long as you escape with spiritual life and health and come up out of all your trials the better for them, you may rejoice in tribulations. Thank God when your temptations abound, and be glad when He puts you into the furnace because of the blessing which you are sure to receive from it.

So then, since you know not what may be on the morrow, take you heart, you fearing one, and put your fears away. Do as you have been bidden—delight yourself in the Lord, and He shall give you the desires of your heart. Cast your burden upon the Lord, and He will sustain you. He will never suffer the righteous to be moved. Did not David say, speaking by the Holy Ghost, "Many are the afflictions of the righteous; but the LORD delivereth him out of them all"? I charge you, therefore, to be of good comfort, since you know not what may be on the morrow. This is the message to fearful saints.

"CHEER FOR DESPONDENCY," METROPOLITAN
TABERNACLE PULPIT, NO. 3183 (UNDATED)

JESUS' AGONIZING PRAYER

And they came to a place which was named Gethsemane.
MARK 14:32

Jesus prayed and wrestled with God, and in our time of trouble, our resort must be to prayer. Restrain not prayer at any time, even when the sun shines brightly upon you, but be sure that you pray when the midnight darkness surrounds your spirit. Prayer is most needed in such an hour as that, so be not slack in it but pour out your whole soul in earnest supplication to your God and say to yourself, "Now above all other times I must pray with the utmost intensity." For consider how Jesus prayed in Gethsemane.

He adopted the lowliest posture and manner. He fell on His face, and prayed, saying, "O my Father, if it be possible, let this cup pass from me." What an extraordinary sight! The eternal Son of God had taken upon Himself our nature, and there He lay as low as the very dust out of which our nature was originally formed. There He lay as low as the most unrighteous sinner or the most humble beggar can lie before God.

Then He began to cry to His Father in plain and simple language, but oh! What force He put into the words He used! Thrice He pleaded with His Father, repeating the same petition, and Luke tells us that "being in an agony he prayed more earnestly; and his sweat was as it were great drops of blood falling down to the ground." He was not only in an agony of suffering but in an agony of prayer at the same time.

But while our Lord's prayer in Gethsemane was thus earnest and intense and repeated, it was at the same time balanced with a ready acquiescence in His Father's will: "Nevertheless not as I will, but as thou wilt." So, suffering one, you whose spirit has sunk within you, you who are depressed and well-nigh distracted with grief, may the Holy Spirit help you to do what Jesus did—to pray, to pray alone, to pray with intensity, to pray with importunity, to pray even unto an agony, for this is the way in which you will prevail with God and be brought through your hour of darkness and grief.

"Christ in Gethsemane," Metropolitan Tabernacle Pulpit, No. 3190 (1879)

THE WAYS GOD COMFORTS US

As one whom his mother comforteth, so will I comfort you; and ye shall be comforted in Jerusalem.
ISAIAH 66:13

It is something very delightful to consider that Father, Son, and Spirit all cooperate to give us comfort. I can understand their cooperating to make the world; I can understand their cooperation in the salvation of a soul; but I am astonished at this same united action in so comparatively small a matter as the comfort of believers. Yet the Holy Three seem to think it a great matter that believers should be happy, or they would not work together to cheer disconsolate spirits.

We must understand when God says, "I will comfort you," that He intends that there are divers ways by which He does it. Sometimes He comforts us in the course of providence. We may be the lowest spoke of the wheel now, but by the revolution of time we may be the uppermost before long. We may suffer very acute pains tonight, but by the morning the Master may have assuaged all our pain. The pause between sickness and health may not be very long. If the good physician shall put His healing hands upon us, we shall soon be restored.

How often, when you thought you were coming to your worst, has there been a sudden brightening of the sky! It is a long lane that has no turning, and it is a long trouble that never comes to an end. It is when the sea ebbs as far as it can go that the tide begins to flow, and they say the darkest part of the night is that which is just before the daybreak. When the winter grows very cold and keen, we begin to hope that spring will soon come—and our desperate sorrows, when they reach their worst, are coming to their close.

So let us be of good cheer. There will not be always such a rough sea, poor troubled saint. You shall be out of the Atlantic into the Pacific ere long, and you shall be out of the sea altogether, and away on the *terra firma* of eternal joy before many years have rolled over your head.

"The Tenderness of God's Comfort," Metropolitan Tabernacle Pulpit, No. 3189 (Undated)

WARS WITHIN

What time I am afraid, I will trust in thee.
PSALM 56:3

It is even quite possible for us to find two minds and two wills—two sets of facilities within ourselves clashing and jarring and warring and contending with one another.

I am sure that every Christian here will follow me while, for a moment, I speak upon this singular duplex condition of Christian experience. You remember how the women returned from the sepulchre. They had seen a vision of angels; they had also seen the Lord, and it is said they departed quickly "with fear and great joy"—very fearful, trembling at what they had seen, but very joyful—never so fearful and yet never so joyful before.

And you remember that the disciples, when the Lord Jesus stood in their midst, "believed not for joy." Extraordinary thing! They did believe, or they could not have had the joy. And yet the joy seemed, when it grew out of the belief, to cut away its own roots and "they believed not for joy"—strange, marvelous state of mind, yet common to the Christian. The same thing is true as to our attitude to sin. Have you not found yourself, beloved believer in Jesus Christ, drawn towards an evil thing for a moment, fascinated by it, finding a tendency in the carnal corruption of your nature to go after evil, and yet, at the very same time, you hated yourself that you should give way even for a moment to a thought so vile?

You have felt the desire to go after sin, but yet another self, as it were, struggled with greater force not to go after it. One faculty seems to say, "How sweet that sin would be," yet you have said, "It is gall and bitterness itself." The flesh has loved it, but the spirit has said, "I abominate it, I loathe it," and has cried out to God to prevent the possibility of our being allowed to indulge ourselves in it.

Thus warring and contending with us, the prince of the power of the air, uniting with our own evil nature, has endeavored to drag us down, while the Holy Ghost, co-working with the incorruptible seed which He has imparted in us, has sought to draw us upwards towards holiness, purity, and perfection. It is a wondrous warfare which only the elect of God can understand.

"Faith Hand in Hand with Fear," Metropolitan Tabernacle Pulpit, No. 3253 (Undated)

OUR MOST REASONABLE CONSOLATION

*And we know that all things work together
for good to them that love God, to them who
are the called according to his purpose.*
ROMANS 8:28

It is a sure sign of grace when a man can trust in his God, for the natural man, when afraid, falls back on some human trust—or he thinks that he will be able to laugh at the occasion of fear. He gives himself up to jollity and forgetfulness, or perhaps he braces himself up with a natural resolution,

> *To take arms against a sea of troubles,*
> *And by opposing end them.*

He goes anywhere but to his God. Only the gracious spirit—only the soul renewed by the Holy Ghost—will say, " 'What time I am afraid,' my one and only resort shall be this, 'I will trust in thee.' " And after all, is it not the most reasonable thing in the world that a soul that is afraid should trust in God? Where can there be a firmer ground of reliance than in Him whose power never can be defeated, whose wisdom is never at a nonplus? If I have God's promise that He will help me, to whom or whither should I go but unto the God who has so promised?

If, in addition, He has given me His oath, "that by two

immutable things, in which it is impossible for God to lie," I might have strong consolation—where shall my timid spirit go but to the shadow of the wings of the God of the covenant who, by promise and by oath, has guaranteed my safety? What are my circumstances? Has He not given me a promise suitable to them, a special promise for each special time?

So I need never be afraid because of my circumstances. Has He not, indeed, given me one text which covers them all with its broad expanse? "We know that all things work together for good to them that love God, to them who are the called according to his purpose." With a God who is almighty and eternally faithful, with a God who promises and seals the promise with His oath that He will help me when I call upon Him—what can be more reasonable than that, when I am afraid, I should come and put my trust in Him?

"FAITH HAND IN HAND WITH FEAR," METROPOLITAN TABERNACLE PULPIT, NO. 3253 (UNDATED)

THROUGH GOOD
TIMES AND BAD

*In God I will praise his word, in God I have put my
trust; I will not fear what flesh can do unto me.*
PSALM 56:4

Dear brethren and sisters, let me exhort you—and may
God's Holy Spirit back up the exhortation!—to the exercise
of a holy trust in God, not only when you are happy but
when you are afraid. Faith in God is a seasonable thing as
well as a reasonable thing. Fruit is always best in its season,
and the time for faith is the time of trial. Faith is never so
full-flavored as when it is produced beneath cloudy skies.
Other fruits need the sun to ripen them, but this is one of
the precious fruits put forth by the moon.

You shall, when your experience is most trying, honor
God the most if you can then trust Him. Surely it needs little
faith to believe in providence when the purse is full. What
sort of faith is it that believes in the merits of the precious
blood of Jesus when it feels its own sanctification to be
complete, if such can ever be the case? What kind of faith
is that which leans on the Beloved when it can stand alone?

But that is true faith which, when it cannot stand by
itself, which sees death written upon all its own power, which
sees almost all its hopes withered and blasted with the east
wind, yet cries, "My God, it is enough! My soul waits only

upon You. My expectation is from You." This is the way to honor God indeed.

Observe the graduation there often is in Christian experience. You will sometimes find believers in so low a state that their heart is full of fear. By and by they are enabled to exercise the faith that God has given them, but it is mingled fear and trust. But they do not stop there—they get a little further (as David did in this Psalm) where it gets to be trust and no fear. "In God have I put my trust: I will not be afraid what man can do unto me." May you climb the steps of that gracious ladder! May you, if you have fear, also have faith with your fear—and then afterwards have your faith without any fear! When faith gets strong enough, fears are expelled.

"Faith Hand in Hand with Fear," Metropolitan Tabernacle Pulpit, No. 3253 (Undated)

FEAR-KILLING FAITH

Jesus saith unto them, Believe ye that I am able to do this?
MATTHEW 9:28

[Jesus] did not say to [the blind men], "Have you feared whether you would ever have your sight? Have you been frightened at the thought that you may have to grope about in darkness and poverty all your days? Have you been in such despair that you have almost feared that you would commit suicide unless your blindness could be cured?" No, Christ did not ask any such questions as these. His one inquiry was "Believe ye that I am able to do this?"

Friends tell us sometimes about the terrors they have experienced before they came to Christ by simple faith, but it would be quite wrong on our part to conclude that such terrors are necessary. I believe that they are never necessary, and that they are seldom useful. It certainly cannot be right to put them in the place of faith in Christ.

Dear friend, I wish that you would answer the Master's question and leave all other matters alone until He asks you about them. He does not question you concerning your fears and your terrors, the plowing and harrowing law work of which some brethren are so fond of talking. His first question is "Believest thou that I am able to do this?" Give Him an answer, and may the Holy Spirit enable you to give the right reply, "Yea, Lord," even as the blind men did when

Christ put a similar question to them! O sinner, how glad and thankful I should be if I knew that you were saying in your heart, "I do believe that Christ is both able and willing to save me, and I cast myself into His arms now."

If you have really done that, you are saved—and now you know and feel and rejoice in His power to save all those who come unto God by Him. Trust in Jesus, for this is the vital sign by which we discern those who are chosen of the Father, regenerated by the Holy Spirit, and redeemed by the precious blood of Jesus. If you truly believe in Jesus, you are born of God; you need not fear that you shall ever perish, but you may even now rejoice with joy unspeakable and full of glory.

"Faith in Christ's Ability," Metropolitan
Tabernacle Pulpit, No. 3302 (1866)

A CURE FOR DEPRESSION

The oil of joy for mourning.
ISAIAH 61:3

Come, beloved, we have at this moment reason for joy—and let us use it.

For, first, let all believers recollect that we have today the joy of the atonement. "By whom also," says the apostle, "we have received the atonement." The atonement will be no more ours in heaven than it is now. "We have redemption by his blood." Our sin will be no more put away in glory than it is at this moment, for our iniquity is even now cast into the depths of the sea. Our substitute has finished transgression and made an end of sin, and having believed in Him, we know that for us the full atonement is already made and the utmost ransom forever paid. "It is finished."

"Therefore being justified by faith, we have peace with God." "There is therefore now no condemnation to them which are in Christ Jesus." Having believed, we know that our sin is as far removed from us as the east is from the west. We also know that the righteousness of Christ is imputed to us and that it covers us from head to foot. This is a divinely sweet ingredient of the oil of joy, which now distills upon us from the head of our glorified Aaron and perfumes even those who are as the skirts of his garments.

Besides that, my brothers, at the present moment we live

in the love of God. It may not be at this moment sensibly shed abroad in your heart by the Holy Ghost, but still, "the Father himself loveth you." If you are a believer in Christ, He will not love you more when you are in heaven than He loves you now, for He loves you infinitely at this instant. You are even now, "accepted in the Beloved." "Beloved, now are we the sons of God."

Infinite love, eternal love, unchanging love, almighty love is the present possession of the children of God. Hence comes our safety; hence comes the certainty of the supply of all our wants—hence, indeed, flow all our joys. At this moment, despite our spirit depression and soul battling and heart strife, the Lord has set His love upon us and rests in that love. Should not this make our faces to shine?

"The Oil of Joy for Mourning," Metropolitan Tabernacle Pulpit, No. 3341 (Undated)

WHEN ANSWERS DON'T COME

O my God, I cry in the day time, but thou hearest not; and in the night season, and am not silent.
Psalm 22:2

Oh! If this is the dark suggestion of the evil one, "Forsake the closet. Give up private devotion. Never draw near to God, for prayer is all a fancy"—I pray you, spurn the thought with all your might and still cry, both in the daytime and at night, for the Lord will still hear your prayer.

And while you never cease from your trust nor from your prayer, grow more earnest in both. Let your faith be still more resolved to give up all dependence anywhere but upon God, and let your cry grow more and more vehement. It is not every knock at mercy's gate that will open it. He who would prevail must handle the knocker well and dash it down again and again and again. As the old Puritan says, "Cold prayers ask for a denial, but it is red-hot prayers which prevail." Bring your prayers as some ancient battering ram against the gate of heaven and force it open with a sacred violence, "for the kingdom of heaven suffereth violence, and the violent take it by storm."

And yet again, cease not to hope. "Go again," said Elijah to his servant seven times. It must have been weary work to the prophet to have to wait so long. He did not stand up once and pray to God as on Carmel and then instantly came down the fire to continue the sacrifice, but again and again, and getting more humble in posture, with his face between his knees, he beseeches the Lord not for fire, which was an unusual thing, but for water, which is the common boon of the skies.

And yet, though he pleads for that which the Lord Himself had promised, yet it did not at once come—and when his servant came back, four, five, six times, the answer was still the same. There was no sign of rain, but the brazen heavens looked down on an earth which was parched as if in an oven. "Go again!" said the prophet, and at the seventh time, lo! There appeared the cloud like unto a man's hand and this cloud was the sure forerunner of the deluge and storm.

"Unanswered Prayer," Metropolitan
Tabernacle Pulpit, No. 3344 (1866)

GOD KNOWS THE FUTURE

But now, O Lord, thou art our father; we are the clay,
and thou our potter; and we all are the work of thy hand.
Isaiah 64:8

Oh! Christian! If you could get rid of the trouble in which you now are, you would not be able to comfort poor mourners as you shall yet do. You would not be a full-grown, strong man if you had not these stern trials to develop your manly vigor. Men do not learn to be intrepid sailors by staying on dry land. You are to put out to sea in the midst of the storm, that you may learn how to manage and guide the vessel of your soul. You are going through a rough drill that you may be a valiant and stalwart, a good soldier of Jesus Christ, for battles are yet to come and grim foes yet to face, for you have many fightings between now and the blessed active ease of heaven.

You have not yet won the crown, but you will have to cut your way inch by inch and foot by foot—and the Master is making you an athlete, that wrestling with your enemies you may overcome. He is strengthening your muscles and tendons, thews and sinews, by the arduous exercise of unanswered prayer that you may be finely useful in the future.

Still, yet again, perhaps the reason why prayer is not always quickly answered is this—a reason which no tongue can tell, but which is inscrutable lying in the sovereign purposes and wisdom of God. Who am I that I should question Him as to what He does? Who am I that I should arraign my Maker before my bar, and say unto Him, "What doest Thou?"

Almighty potter, You have a right to do as You will with Your own clay! We have learned to submit to Your will not because we must, but because we love that will, feeling that Your will is the highest good of Your creatures and the sublimest wisdom. Why should we be so anxious to know the depth of the sea, which cannot be fathomed by our line? Why must we be toiling to heave the lead so often? Leave these things with God and go on with your praying and your believing, and all shall yet be well with you.

"UNANSWERED PRAYER," METROPOLITAN
TABERNACLE PULPIT, NO. 3344 (1866)

GOD THINKS OF YOU

*But I am poor and needy; yet the L*ORD *thinketh upon me.*
PSALM 40:17

There are some who cry, "I am poor and needy; woe is me that I should be so. But the Lord does not think of me. I have looked up to heaven, but no eye of pity looks down upon me in the depth of my misery." Many a wretched mind, many a bereaved spirit, many a downcast heart has cried, "The Lord has forgotten me. He counts the number of the stars and calls them by their names, but as for me, I am too little, too insignificant, too obscure—I cannot believe that God thinks upon me."

Dear friend, I pray that you may not only be able to join in one half of my text by saying, "I am poor and needy," but that you may humbly unite in the second declaration, "yet the LORD thinketh upon me." Despite your insignificance and unworthiness, you may yet learn that the Lord has thoughts of love towards you and is causing all things to work together for your external, internal, and eternal good.

Do not let it surprise you that one of old should say, "I am poor and needy; yet the LORD thinketh upon me," for God has often thought of poor and needy persons. Look at Joseph when he was in prison and the iron entered into his soul—his reputation was gone and he was reproached and even punished unjustly, yet we read that the Lord was with

181

Joseph. And in due time He brought him out and set him on the throne of Egypt.

So Ruth, the Moabitess, came penniless to Israel's land, and she went to glean among the sheaves as a poor and needy peasant woman. But the Lord was thinking upon her and so provided for her that she rose to an honorable estate—and her name is written among the progenitors of our Lord Jesus.

To give you a more modern instance—the apostles were poor fishermen with their little boats and well-worn nets, upon the Lake of Galilee; yet the Lord looked upon them, unlearned and ignorant men as they were, and made them to be the pioneers of His kingdom. Never mind how poor and needy you are. You may yet be heirs of God, joint heirs with Jesus Christ.

"SUNLIGHT FOR CLOUDY DAYS," METROPOLITAN
TABERNACLE PULPIT, NO. 3345 (UNDATED)

WORRY NOT—
GOD'S MERCY IS FOR YOU

*I will have mercy on whom I will have mercy, and I will
have compassion on whom I will have compassion.*
ROMANS 9:15

Again, if it should seem difficult to you for God to think
upon the poor and needy, I invite you to answer the question
"Who need God's thoughts most?" On the field of battle,
after the fight, if a surgeon should be there to attend to the
wounded, where will he go first? Of course, he will go to
those whose gaping wounds have almost opened the gates
of death for them, and the slightly wounded he will leave
till he has more time.

If I see a physician's carriage hurrying down the street, I
feel morally certain that he is not driving to my door, for I
am not dangerously ill. But if I know of one who has fallen
in a fit, or has been badly injured by an accident, I conclude
that he is going to him. When the angel of mercy is made
to fly very swiftly, be you sure that he is speeding to one who
is in urgent need of grace.

Remember, too, that God has always dealt with men
from that point of view. When God made His election of
men, or ever the earth was, He chose them as fallen and
undeserving that He might lift them up to the praise of
the glory of His grace. His choice of men was never guided

by anything good that He saw in them. As says the apostle Paul, "For the children being not yet born, neither having done any good or evil, that the purpose of God according to election might stand, not of works, but of him that calleth."

The decree still stands: "I will have mercy on whom I will have mercy, and I will have compassion on whom I will have compassion." The Lord of grace asks in His sovereignty, "Shall I not do as I will with my own?" God views men as all guilty, and finding them guilty, He yet chooses unto Himself a people in whom His grace shall be resplendent. Therefore do not conclude that He will pass you by because you are poor and needy.

<hr />

"SUNLIGHT FOR CLOUDY DAYS," METROPOLITAN
TABERNACLE PULPIT, NO. 3345 (UNDATED)

FAITH: BETTER THAN FRETTING

Cast thy burden upon the Lord, and he shall sustain thee: he shall never suffer the righteous to be moved.
PSALM 55:22

They tell me that if a man were to fall into the sea, he would float if he would remain quiet—but because he struggles he sinks. I am sure it is so when we are in affliction. Fretfulness results in weakening us, in hiding from us wise methods of relief, and in general in doubling our pains. It is folly to kick against the pricks. It is wisdom to kiss the rod. Trust more and fear less.

If you have trusted your soul with Christ, can you not trust Him with everything else? Can you not trust Him with your sick child, with your wealth, with your business, with your life? "Oh," says one, "I hardly like to do that. It is almost presumption to take our minor cares to the great Lord." But in so doing you will prove the truthfulness of your faith!

I heard of a man who was walking along the high road with a pack on his back. He was growing weary and was, therefore, glad when a gentleman came along in a chaise and asked him to take a seat with him. The gentleman noticed that he kept his pack strapped to his shoulders and so he said, "Why do you not put your pack down?" "Why, sir," said the traveler, "I did not venture to impose. It was very kind of you to take me up, and I could not expect you to carry my pack as well." "Why," said his friend, "do you not see that whether your pack is on your back or off your back, I have to carry it?"

Why do you weary yourself with care when God cares for you? If I were afraid of burglars and kept a watchman to guard my house at night, I certainly should not sit up all night myself. The Lord is your keeper—why are you fearful? It is infinitely better that you should be able to say, "The Lord thinketh upon me," than that you should have all power and wisdom and wealth in your own hands. I charge you, then, to rest in the Lord and fret no longer.

"Sunlight for Cloudy Days," Metropolitan Tabernacle Pulpit, No. 3345 (Undated)

IN GOD'S HANDS

Behold, God is my salvation; I will trust, and not
be afraid: for the LORD JEHOVAH is my strength
and my song; he also is become my salvation.
ISAIAH 12:2

I know of nothing more delightful to the believer than every morning to commit the day's troubles to God and then go down into the world feeling, "Well, my Father knows it all."

You know, perhaps, the good old story which is told of the woman on shipboard who was greatly afraid in a storm—but she saw her husband perfectly at peace and she could not understand it. Her husband said he would tell her the reason, so snatching up a sword, he pointed it at her heart. She looked at it, but did not tremble. "Well," he said, "are you not afraid? The sword is sharp and I could kill you in a moment." "No," she said, "because it is in your hands!" "Ah," he replied, "and that is why I am not afraid, because the storm is in my Father's hands and He loves me better than I love you."

A little child was at play in a lower room; and as he played away by himself, amusing himself, about every ten minutes he ran to the foot of the stairs and called out, "Mother, are you there?" and his mother answered, "Yes, I am here," and the little lad went back to his sport and fun—and was as happy as happy could be—and until again it crossed his mind that his mother might have gone. So he ran to the stairs again and called, "Mother, are you there?" "All right," she said, and as soon as he heard her voice again, back he went once more to his play.

It is just so with us. In times of temporal trouble, we go to the mercy seat in prayer and we say, "Father, are You there? Is it Your hand that is troubling me? Is it Your providence that has sent me this difficulty?" And as soon as you hear the voice which says, "It is I," you are no longer afraid. Oh! Happy are they who, when they are afraid in this way, trust in the Lord.

"FEARING AND TRUSTING—TRUSTING AND NOT FEARING,"
METROPOLITAN TABERNACLE PULPIT, NO. 3362 (1867)

SALVATION ANXIETY

For I am persuaded, that neither death, nor life,
nor angels, nor principalities, nor powers, nor things
present, nor things to come, nor height, nor depth,
nor any other creature, shall be able to separate us from
the love of God, which is in Christ Jesus our Lord.
Romans 8:38–39

Among the best and most careful of believers this fear intrudes itself, "Lest, after having preached to others, I myself should be a castaway." Lest, after having been united to the church, I should prove to be a dead member and so be cut out of the living vine.

But when you and I are besieged by these doubts and fears—and I very often am—as to whether we are the children of God or not, what is the best thing for us to do? "What time I am afraid, I will trust in thee." This is the shortcut with the devil. This is the way to cut off his head more readily than anyhow else.

Go straight away to Christ. Do not stop to argue with Satan. He is a crafty old liar and he will be sure to defeat you if it comes to argument between you. Say to him, "Satan, if I be deceived, if all I have ever known up till now has been only head knowledge, if I am nothing but a mere hypocrite, yet now,

> *Black, I to the fountain fly;*
> *Wash me, Savior, or I die.*

It is a blessed thing to begin again—to be always beginning and yet always going on—for no man ever goes on to perfection who forgets his first love, his first faith, and forgets to walk in Christ Jesus as he walked in Him at the first.

Beloved, whatever may be the doubt that comes to you tonight, I beseech you recollect it is still "him that cometh unto me I will in no wise cast out." If you have been a backslider, weep over it. If you have been a great sinner, be sorry for it—but still remember, "All manner of sin and of blasphemy shall be forgiven unto men," and "Where sin abounded, grace doth much more abound."

Come, come, come, you doubting one, trembling and broken to pieces. Come again—a guilty, weak and helpless worm—and cast yourself into Jesus' arms.

"FEARING AND TRUSTING—TRUSTING AND NOT FEARING,"
METROPOLITAN TABERNACLE PULPIT, NO. 3362 (1867)

CONSOLING COMPASSION

He was moved with compassion.
MATTHEW 9:36

Now I do not know a single infirmity that I have or that you have, my Christian brother, but what Christ Jesus has been moved with compassion about it and has provided for it. He has not left one single weak point of which we have to say, "There I shall fail, because He will not help there," but He has looked us over and over from head to foot and said, "You will have an infirmity there; I will provide for it. You will have a weakness there; I will provide for it."

And oh! How His promises meet every case! Did you ever get into a corner where there was not a promise in the corner too? Had you ever to pass through a river but there was a promise about His being in the river with you? Were you ever on the sick bed without a promise like this: "I will make thy bed in thy sickness"? In the midst of pestilence have you not found a promise that "he shall cover thee with his feathers, and under his wings shalt thou trust"? The Lord's great compassion has met the wants of all His servants to the end.

If our children should ever need as much patience to be exercised towards them as Christ needs to exercise towards us, I am sure there would be none of us able to bear the house. They have their infirmities and they full often vex and grieve us, it may be, but oh! We ought to have much compassion for the infirmities of our children—ay, and of our brethren and sisters and neighbors—for what compassion has the Lord had with us? I do believe none but God could bear with such untoward children as we ourselves are. He sees our faults, you know, when we do not see them and He knows what those faults are more thoroughly than we do. Yet still He never smites in anger. He cuts us not off, but He still continues to show us abounding mercies.

Oh! What a guardian Savior is the Lord Jesus Christ to us—and how we ought to bless His name at all times and how His praise should be continually in our mouth.

"The Compassion of Jesus," Metropolitan
Tabernacle Pulpit, No. 3438 (Undated)

COMFORT IS NEVER OUT OF REACH

*Come unto me, all ye that labour and are
heavy laden, and I will give you rest.*
MATTHEW 11:28

Oh! The comforts that He gives on a sickbed! Oh! The consolations of Christ when you are very low. If there is anything dainty to the taste in the Word of God, you get it then. If there be any bowels of mercy, you hear them sounding for you then. When you are in the saddest plight, Christ comes to your aid with the sweetest manifestations, for He is moved with compassion.

How frequently have I noticed—and I tell it to His praise, for though it shows my weakness, it proves His compassion—that sometimes, after preaching the gospel, I have been so filled with self-reproach that I could hardly sleep through the night because I had not preached as I desired. I have sat me down and cried over some sermons, as though I knew that I had missed the mark and lost the opportunity. Not once nor twice, but many a time has it happened, that within a few days someone has come to tell me that he or she found the Lord through that very sermon, the shortcoming of which I had deplored.

Glory be to Jesus, it was His gentleness that did it. He did not want His servant to be too much bowed down with a sense of infirmity and so He had compassion on him and comforted him. Have not you noticed, some of you, that after doing your best to serve the Lord, when somebody has sneered at you or you have met with such a rebuff as made you half inclined to give up the work, an unexpected success has been given you so that you have not played the Jonah and ran away to Tarshish, but kept to your work? Ah! How many times in your life, if you could read it all, you would have to stop and write between the lines, "He was moved with compassion."

Many and many a time, when no other compassion could help, when all the sympathy of friends would be unavailing, He has been moved with compassion towards us—has said to us, "Be of good cheer," banished our fears with the magic of His voice, and filled our souls to overflowing with gratitude.

"THE COMPASSION OF JESUS," METROPOLITAN
TABERNACLE PULPIT, No. 3438 (UNDATED)

GOD NEVER REJECTS OUR PLEAS

For ye know the grace of our Lord Jesus Christ,
that, though he was rich, yet for your sakes he became
poor, that ye through his poverty might be rich.

2 CORINTHIANS 8:9

Believe me: there is nothing sweeter to a forlorn and broken spirit than the fact that Jesus has compassion. Are any of you sad and lonely? Have any of you been cruelly wronged? Have you lost the goodwill of some you esteemed? Do you seem as if you had the cold shoulder even from good people? Do not say, in the anguish of your spirit, "I am lost," and give up. He has compassion on you.

And you, broken down in health and broken down in fortune, scarcely with shoes for your feet, you are welcome in the house of God—welcome as the most honored guest in the assembly of the saints. Let not the weighty grief that hangs over your soul tempt you to think that hopeless darkness have settled your fate and foreclosed your doom. Though your sin may have beggared you, Christ can enrich you with better riches. He has compassion.

"Ah!" say you, "they will pass me on the stairs. They will give me a broad pathway, and if they see me in the street they will not speak to me—even His disciples will not." Be it so, but better than His disciples, tenderer by far is Jesus.

Is there a man here whom to associate with were a scandal from which the pure and pious would shrink? The holy, harmless, undefiled one will not disdain even him—for this man receiveth sinners—He is a friend of publicans and sinners.

He is never happier than when He is relieving and retrieving the forlorn, the abject, and the outcast. He despises not any that confess their sins and seek His mercy. No pride nestles in His dear heart, no sarcastic word rolls off His gracious tongue, no bitter expression falls from His blessed lips. He still receives the guilty.

Pray to Him now. Now let the silent prayer go up, "My Savior, have pity upon me; be moved with compassion towards me, for if misery is any qualification for mercy, I am a fit object for Thy compassion. Oh! Save me for Thy mercy's sake!"

"THE COMPASSION OF JESUS," METROPOLITAN
TABERNACLE PULPIT, NO. 3438 (UNDATED)

196

OUR GREATEST COMFORT

But the Comforter, which is the Holy Ghost,
whom the Father will send in my name, he shall
teach you all things, and bring all things to your
remembrance, whatsoever I have said unto you.
JOHN 14:26

We will remark that God the Holy Ghost is a very loving comforter. I am in distress and want consolation. Some passerby hears of my sorrow and he steps within, sits down and essays to cheer me. He speaks soothing words, but he loves me not—he is a stranger, he knows me not at all, he has only come in to try his skill, and what is the consequence? His words run o'er me like oil upon a slab of marble—they are like the pattering rain upon the rock. They do not break my grief; it stands unmoved as adamant, because he has no love for me.

But let someone who loves me dearly as his own life come and plead with me, then truly his words are music. They taste like honey. He knows the password of the doors of my heart, and my ear is attentive to every word. I catch the intonation of each syllable as it falls, for it is like the harmony of the harps of heaven.

Oh! There is a voice in love. It speaks a language which is its own; it is an idiom and an accent which none can mimic—wisdom cannot imitate it, oratory cannot attain unto it. It is love alone which can reach the mourning heart; love is the only handkerchief which can wipe the mourner's tears away. And is not the Holy Ghost a loving comforter?

Do you know, O saint, how much the Holy Spirit loves you? Can you measure the love of the Spirit? Do you know how great is the affection of His soul towards you? Go, measure heaven with your span. Go, weigh the mountains in the scales. Go, take the ocean's water and tell each drop. Go, count the sand upon the sea's wide shore, and when you have accomplished this, you can tell how much He loves you. He has loved you long, He has loved you well, He loved you ever, and He still shall love you. Surely He is the person to comfort you, because He loves. Admit Him, then, to your heart, O Christian, that He may comfort you in your distress.

"THE COMFORTER," THE NEW PARK
STREET PULPIT, NO. 5 (1855)

HE SILENCES EVERY FEAR

Let us therefore come boldly unto the
throne of grace, that we may obtain mercy,
and find grace to help in time of need.
HEBREWS 4:16

He is a faithful comforter. Love sometimes proves unfaithful. "Oh! Sharper than a serpent's tooth" is an unfaithful friend! Oh! Far more bitter than the gall of bitterness, to have a friend to turn from me in my distress! Oh! Woe of woes, to have one who loves me in my prosperity forsake me in the dark days of my trouble.

Sad, indeed, but such is not God's Spirit. He ever loves and loves even to the end—a faithful comforter. Child of God, you are in trouble. A little while ago you found Him a sweet and loving comforter; you obtained relief from Him when others were but broken cisterns. He sheltered you in His bosom and carried you in His arms.

Oh, wherefore do you distrust Him now? Away with your fears! for He is a faithful comforter. "Ah! But," you say, "I fear I shall be sick and shall be deprived of His ordinances." Nevertheless, He shall visit you on your sickbed and sit by your side to give you consolation. "Ah! But I have distresses greater than you can conceive of; wave upon wave rolls over me, deep calls unto deep at the noise of the Eternal's waterspouts." Nevertheless, He will be faithful to His promise.

"Ah! But I have sinned." So you have, but sin cannot sever you from His love—He loves you still. Think not, O poor downcast child of God, because the scars of your old sins have marred your beauty that He loves you less because of that blemish Oh, no! He loved you when He foreknew your sin. He loved you with the knowledge of what the aggregate of your wickedness would be, and He does not love the less now.

Come to Him in all boldness of faith. Tell Him you have grieved Him, and He will forget your wandering and will receive you again. The kisses of His love shall be bestowed upon you, and the arms of His grace shall embrace you. He is faithful—trust Him, He will never deceive you—trust Him, He will never leave you.

"THE COMFORTER," THE NEW PARK
STREET PULPIT, NO. 5 (1855)

NEEDLESS FEARS

I, even I, am he that comforteth you: who art thou,
that thou shouldest be afraid of a man that shall die,
and of the son of man which shall be made as grass;
and forgettest the LORD thy maker, that hath stretched
forth the heavens, and laid the foundations of the
earth; and hast feared continually every day because
of the fury of the oppressor, as if he were ready to
destroy? and where is the fury of the oppressor?
ISAIAH 51:12–13

I want to speak upon this point—that many fears, which are
entertained by good men and women, are really groundless.

Thou "hast feared continually every day because of the
fury of the oppressor, as if he were ready to destroy. . .and
where is the fury of the oppressor?" The probable meaning
of this verse is that the oppressor never came, so that they
never did feel the force of his fury—and in like manner,
many of God's people are constantly under apprehensions
of calamities which will never occur to them. They suffer
far more in merely dreading them than they would have to
endure if they actually came upon them.

In their imagination, there are rivers in their way—and
they are anxious to know how they shall wade through them
or swim across them. There are no such rivers in existence, but
they are agitated and distressed about them. Our old proverb

says, "Don't cross the bridge till you come to it," but these timid people are continually crossing bridges that only exist in their foolish fancies. They stab themselves with imaginary daggers, they starve themselves in imaginary famines, and even bury themselves in imaginary graves. Such strange creatures are we that we probably smart more under blows which never fall upon us than we do under those which do actually come. The rod of God does not smite us as sharply as the rod of our own imagination does; our groundless fears are our chief tormentors, and when we are enabled to abolish our self-inflictions, all the inflictions of the world become light enough.

It is a pity, however, that any who are taught of God and who have had faith in Christ given to them should fall into so guilty, and at the same time, so painful a habit as this of fearing the oppressor who does not come, and who never will come.

"Needless Fears," Metropolitan Tabernacle Pulpit, No. 3098 (1874)

GOD IS GREATER THAN OUR FEARS

For I the LORD thy God will hold thy right hand,
saying unto thee, Fear not; I will help thee.
ISAIAH 41:13

You have fears with regard to a great trouble that threatens you. Well, will it separate you from the love of Christ? If you cannot answer that question, let Paul answer it for you: "I am persuaded, that neither death, nor life, nor angels, nor principalities, nor powers, nor things present, nor things to come, nor height, nor depth, nor any other creature, shall be able to separate us from the love of God, which is in Christ Jesus our Lord." You say that your enemies slander you, but will Christ believe them? They are trying to take away your character, but will your Lord think any the less of you? Will He be deceived by their falsehoods? You say that friends are forsaking you, but will they take Jesus away and make Him forsake you?

You say that your enemies are doing all that they can to destroy you, but can they destroy the divine promises? The Lord has promised to give unto His sheep eternal life—can they take that promise from you or make it of no value? They may frown at you, but can they keep you out of heaven? They may threaten you, but can they make the covenant of grace to be of no effect? While eternal things are safe, we may well be content to let other things come or go just as God wills.

Again, can anyone do anything to you which God does not permit? And if God permits it, can any real harm come to you? "Who is he that will harm you, if ye be followers of that which is good?" "We know that all things work together for good to them that love God, to them who are the called according to his purpose." Then how can anything work for your hurt if you are really the Lord's? Can anyone curse those whom God blesses?

"Needless Fears," Metropolitan Tabernacle Pulpit, No. 3098 (1874)

AWAY WITH FEAR

*Fear thou not; for I am with thee: be not
dismayed; for I am thy God: I will strengthen
thee; yea, I will help thee; yea, I will uphold thee
with the right hand of my righteousness.*
Isaiah 41:10

Five times in this verse you get some form of the pronoun *thou*, and five times you get the pronoun *I*. Whatever there may be of you, there shall be as much of God. Whatever there may be of your weakness, there shall be as much of God's strength. Whatever there may be of your sin, there shall be as much of God's mercy to meet it all.

"Fear thou not; for I am with thee." Many a man fears because he is afraid of loneliness. More or less we must be alone in the service of God. Christian companionship is a great comfort, but if a man becomes a leader in Israel, he becomes a lonely spirit to a certain degree. So too in suffering, there is a bitterness with which no stranger can intermeddle. A part of the road to heaven every man must tread with no companion but his God.

"O taste and see that the LORD is good." Do not merely "see" that He is good as you read the text, but "taste" the text. Let it lie on the palate of your soul. Absorb it into your very nature. Try to know that it is true, and true to you, though you are the very least of God's people in your own estimation and the most unworthy sinner this side of hell. "Fear thou not; for I am with thee: be not dismayed; for I am thy God: I will strengthen thee; yea, I will help thee; yea, I will uphold thee with the right hand of my righteousness."

Go home, and take the text with you in the hand of faith. It shall prove to you like the widow's barrel of meal and cruse of oil. It shall not fail you till the day when the Lord shall bring you out of this land of famine to eat bread in His kingdom with His dear Son.

O come to the tree of the cross, and look up to His sufferings, and rely upon Him. And then, when you have sat under His shadow with great delight, may this text, which is one of the fruits of that tree, be sweet unto your taste.

***

"Away with Fear," Metropolitan Tabernacle Pulpit, No. 930 (1870)

MORE FROM
CHARLES SPURGEON

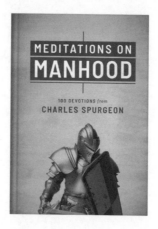

Charles Spurgeon, "the Prince of Preachers," is well remembered and remarkably readable some 130 years after his death. Now, this devotional for men has been compiled from his decades of weekly sermons. You'll find deep yet accessible teaching on biblical manhood, as Spurgeon distills godly principles for men of all ages.

Hardcover / ISBN 978-1-63609-719-0

Find This and More from Barbour
Publishing at Your Favorite Bookstore
or www.barbourbooks.com

BARBOUR
PUBLISHING